FROM ABSENCE TO ATTENDANCE

D1128543

Alastair Evans is course director of the Diploma in Personnel Management and senior lecturer in human resource management at Thames Valley University, Ealing. He holds the degree of MA in industrial relations from the University of Warwick and is a Fellow of the CIPD. Prior to his current post, he was a personnel director in the computer software industry and, before that, a consultant in the same industry. He also worked for the (former) Institute of Personnel Management for a number of years as a policy adviser in the field of employee resourcing. He has published a dozen books over the last 20 years on such topics as human resource planning, computerised personnel systems, data protection, and flexible work patterns; this is his third book co-authored with Steve Palmer.

Steve Palmer began his industrial relations career as assistant research officer with the National Union of Seaman. He left to study for a master's degree at the London School of Economics, and later joined Incomes Data Services as a senior researcher on pay and conditions. In 1979 he started at the (then) Institute of Personnel Management as policy adviser on pay and employment conditions, a post he held for 11 years before becoming the Institute's Assistant Director – Development. In 1992 he was appointed deputy director of employment affairs with the Conferderation of British Industry. He is now remuneration adviser at the Office of Manpower Economics. He lives in South London with his wife and two cats.

Other titles in the series:

The Chartered Institute of Personnel and Development is the leading publisher of books and reports for personnel and training professionals, students, and for all those concerned with the effective management and development of people at work. For details of all our titles, please contact the Publishing Department:

tel. 020-8263 3387
fax 020-8263 3850
e-mail us on publish@cipd.co.uk
The catalogue of all CIPD titles can be viewed on the CIPD website:
www.cipd.co.uk/publications

FROM ABSENCE TO ATTENDANCE

Alastair Evans and Steve Palmer

Chartered Institute of Personnel and Development

First published in 1997

Reprinted 1999, 2000

Design by Paperweight
Typeset by Action Publishing Technology, Gloucester
Printed in Great Britain by
The Cromwell Press, Wiltshire

British Library Cataloguing in Publication Data
A catalogue record for this book is available from the British Library

ISBN 0-85292-706-1

Chartered Institute of Personnel and Development, CIPD House, Camp Road, London SW19 4UX
Tel: 020-8971 9000   Fax: 020-8263 3333
E-mail: cipd@cipd.co.uk
Website: www.cipd.co.uk
Incorporated by Royal Charter. Registered charity no. 1079797.

CONTENTS

ACKNOWLEDGEMENTS

The authors would like to record their special thanks Barbara Duffner, Director Personnel, Royal Mail Scotland and Northern Ireland, Andreas Ghosh, London Borough of Lewisham, and Mel Lambert, Group Personnel Director, Fiat UK Ltd, for kindly checking and agreeing the case-study mat-erial. We are also grateful to our editor Matthew Reisz for his many suggestions for improving the text – any errors that remain are solely ours; to Susan Anderson of the CBI for her help and advice; and to the CIPD's Library and Information Service for cheerfully carrying out a lot of the spadework.

INTRODUCTION

Today and every working day of the year, something like a million people in Britain fail to turn up at work because of absence, either self- or medically certificated, or indeed uncertificated. Though it depends on the time of year, on average a further three million will be on holiday and a further number will be on leave for some other authorised reason. In the region of 200 million days are lost each year through absence, excluding holidays and authorised leave, and the annual cost to the economy has been estimated at £12 billion a year. To an organisation employing 1,000 people with an annual absence rate of 5 per cent and a salary bill close to average national pay rates, the annual cost of absence to this organisation will be close to £1 million. Despite these high costs, surveys by the CBI and the Industrial Society have shown that a quarter of all organisations do not even bother to keep absence statistics, and as many as three quarters have no idea of the cost of absence to their organisation. Because the keeping of absence statistics is usually the responsibility of the human resource (HR) department, where one exists, this apparent lack of concern for what is a major cost for organisations is decidedly worrying.

The essential facts revealed by the national absence surveys are these. The national average rate of absence, in terms of percentage of time lost, is around 3.7 per cent, which represents around eight-and-a-half days per employee per year. There are, however, wide variations in the statistics by occupational group, region and size of firm. Manual workers lose on average close to 10 days per year, while non-manuals lose just under eight. There are also variations between and within industrial sectors that suggest that effective absence management policies and practices can make a difference that will affect an organisation's bottom line. Rates of absence in the public sector are on average 40 per cent higher than in the private sector, but even within the public sector absence performance varies widely. A top-performing government agency may lose only four days a year, while a poor performer loses more than three times as many. The story is much the same in the private sector, although overall absence rates are lower. The best performers are found in construction, chemicals and the professional services sector, in which around two to two-and-a-half days are lost a year, while the worst performer, the food and drink industry, loses up to five times as much, at over 11 days per employee. Even within the food and drink industry, the best performers lose just four days per employee per year.

How can such wide variations be explained – two days lost per employee a year at one end of the scale and nearly a fortnight a year at the other? Of course, employees become ill from time to time, but such differences in absence levels surely cannot be explained by illness alone. Except for certain industries with higher health risks, good or bad health must be assumed to be normally distributed among different employee populations. It is our contention that the difference lies in having top management commitment to absence control, and in the implementation of the appropriate policies and practices. HR practitioners have a major contribution to make in bringing down the absence levels in organisations where they are unacceptably high, and thereby making a significant impact on the cost line. Moreover, we see it as the task of HR professionals to benchmark and target best-practice performance levels, not just to be content with getting absence levels down to the industry average, and to encourage a climate of continuous improvement. If one part of an industry sector can achieve two or three days lost a year, why should another with a similar workforce composition experience three times this number?

This book tackles the issues associated with attendance management in the following way. The essential starting-point is to have accurate and timely data about time lost, frequency of absence, and absence costs. With the appropriate data available, it needs to be monitored and levels of performance fed back to line managers, who perform a vital link in the chain of effective absence management. Moreover, as stated, we need to set targets for achievement by benchmarking against industry-sector best practice or against comparable organisations. These matters are considered in Chapter 1.

Next, we need to understand the nature and causes of our organisation's absence problems; these are covered in Chapter 2. Absence is a complex subject. Its causes are many and varied, but it is essential to analyse the causes in order to devise the appropriate policies. There is no point in introducing policies to tackle a cause of absence that does not exist, or in grafting on policies that may have worked in other places where the nature of the absence problem or the culture of the organisation is completely different.

Chapter 3 reviews the many and varied initiatives that organisations have implemented to tackle their absence problems. Again, we must emphasise that there are no prescriptions, only practical ideas that have worked in some organisations, and the reader needs to view them critically in order to decide how appropriate any of them are for his or her own organisation. Moreover, there is some sense in adopting absence-control strategies that seek to balance both the 'carrot' and the 'stick'. For example, if we are seeking to tighten up on absence-reporting procedures and disciplinary sanctions, this can usefully be balanced by some more positive approaches to absence management. Bear in mind that if the chosen strategy is successful there will be cost savings, some of which can usefully be channelled into policies that support effective absence management, such as flexible working arrangements or employee assistance programmes. At the end of the day the strategy will need to be sold to staff. Too much emphasis on punishment-centred policies may have a negative effect on morale, so these need to be balanced by the introduction of positive measures, many of which are considered in the course of this book.

Chapter 4 provides guidance on the disciplinary and legal framework of absence management. A considerable body of case-law has been established which sets fairly exacting procedures for employers to follow, especially when dealing with the dismissal of long-term sick employees. These requirements, together with the doctrine of frustration in relation to the long-term sick and the vexed question of dealing with the persistent and frequent short-term absentee, are also considered.

The book concludes with an Appendix containing three case-studies of effective absence management in action. In the first case, concerning Iveco Ford Truck, absence among manual workers was brought down by half, from 7 per cent to a targeted rate of 3.5 per cent, compared with an industry average of around 5 per cent. The second case comes from the London Borough of Lewisham which, prior to its implementation of an absence control strategy, had an absence rate of over 19 days per employee per year, a rate of around 8 per cent – over twice the national average for local government. Over a period of time this has been brought down by close to a half of the former rate, and now stands at 10 days per employee – just above 4 per cent. The target is to achieve 3 per cent, and further initiatives are still being implemented. The third case comes from Royal Mail Scotland and Northern Ireland, which lost an average of nearly 15 days per employee through absence, at an estimated annual direct cost of over £11 million. The study describes their initiatives to bring these levels down. Because they are recent, it is too soon to make a definitive assessment of their impact, but the early signs are encouraging.

1

MEASURING, MONITORING AND BENCHMARKING

Tackling sickness absence is one obvious area where the personnel practitioner can point to a clear financial improvement in the bottom line from implementing properly designed and enforced personnel strategies. With the *direct* annual cost to employees of absence put at £533 per employee in 1996, and with evidence that the *indirect* costs could easily double that figure, the scope for savings is substantial. For example, just by reducing its absence rate from 7 per cent to 4 per cent (near to the national average) a company of 500 people with a wage bill of £9 million would save some £250,000 a year.

This book suggests how you too can make a powerful contribution to reducing costs by reducing absence levels in your organisation. You will find in Chapter 3 a wide range of policy options you could adopt in the light, of course, of the causes of absence (Chapter 2) and any legal ramifications of taking action. But the first step to controlling absence (or managing attendance) is measurement. That is what this chapter is all about. Without it you cannot know what absence problem you face or the most appropriate method for dealing with it. The golden rule for controlling absence therefore is *know thine enemy*.

That doesn't just mean know your absence level, but also what it looks like: whether it is short- or long-term, age- or gender-related, restricted to certain departments or individuals, more likely to occur on certain days of the week or months of the year, etc. For example, some absences are potentially much more disruptive than others. A long and foreshadowed absence is easier to handle than a lot of one- or two-day absences taken at little or no notice – even though in terms of days absent the two different forms may amount to the same. And absence amongst your flexible workforce – part-timers, temporaries or seasonal workers who are employed specifically to ensure a tight match between the supply and demand for products and services – can cause more problems than absence amongst full-timers, so a breakdown of the information along those lines could also be useful.

When you think about it, absence is a complex subject. Dealing with it means taking account of the complexities and implementing the right policies.

Measuring absence

The most common method of measuring sickness absence is to calculate the number of lost days/shifts as a proportion of the potential total number of days/shifts worked. This has been termed a 'time-lost measure' and is the approach adopted in most organisations and also by the CBI in its national surveys of sickness absence. The CBI asks respondents for their absence rate assuming a 228-day working year (ie 365 minus weekends, eight public holidays and 25 days' annual leave).

Although this approach is common, however, it is also rather crude and raises some problems. If you are benchmarking against other organisations, you do not know whether their base calculation – or even their definition of absence – is the same as yours. Some organisations use a 365-day year, for instance, while others include annual leave; and because it measures lost time in total, this index tends to over-emphasise long-term sickness in the absence statistics. 'Days' may not be the most appropriate measure of time anyway. For part-time employees, for example, hours lost may be better.

Another approach measures the frequency of absence – that is, the number of separate sicknesses. ACAS (1994) suggests two formulae. The first, the 'frequency rate', measures the average number of spells of absence per employee and is partic-ularly helpful in determining whether time lost is due to lots of short absences or a few long absences. The frequency rate is simply the number of absences in a period divided by the number of employees, multiplied by 100. The formula can be refined to give an 'individual frequency rate' which shows the number of employees absent during a period. In this case the rate is calculated as the number of employees who take one or more periods of absence divided by the total number of employees, multiplied by 100.

Because short-term absences can be more disruptive, a frequency index may be a better measure of the overall impact of absence on your organisation than purely total time lost. It also lends itself to weighting through analyses such as the *Bradford Factor*, an approach devised at the University of Bradford. The approach focuses attention on the frequency of an individual's absence by awarding points in a weighted way which emphasises spells of absence. The full equation is:

$$Points\ scored = (S \times S) \times D$$

where S is the number of spells of absence over a period (typically 12 months) and D equals total days off in the same period. If frequency of absence is the major issue, the Bradford approach allows policies to be triggered on this basis rather than the more normal 'so many days in so many months'. For example, one absence of five days would be awarded, say, 5 points (1×5), but five absences of one day would receive 125 points $(5 \times 5 \times 5)$. We consider trigger points in more detail in Chapter 3.

The problem is that whilst a Bradford-type measure is better for deciding what policies to adopt and when to implement different stages, for the purposes of benchmarking we have to accept that most organisations use a pure time-lost measure. Organisations might therefore find it useful to use a time-lost measure for general external comparisons, but use a frequency-based measure to help design their internal personnel approach to absence management.

Costing absence

A good way to convince senior management that absence ought to be tackled, and to justify to them the need for investment in, for example, computerisation to help monitor absence levels, is to show them the figures. Costing absence is comparatively simple, especially if you stick to the *direct* wage costs, ie the cost of paying employees off sick. (You could also include some other costs if known, for example costs of temporary replacements or additional overtime working – but more indirect costs can require some subjective judgements: how, for instance, can you measure in financial terms a reduced quality of service or poorer customer care, at least in the shorter term? We noted earlier that some organisations were able to give the CBI an estimate of indirect costs, and it was around the direct cost level, but only 11 out of 691 could do so.) So, looking only at the direct wage cost, Hugo Fair (1992) suggests the following sample form for calculating absence costs:

Sample Form for Calculation

Cost of absenteeism

Enter number of employees	———	(a)
Enter average weekly wage	£———	(b)
Multiply (a) × (b)	£———	(c)
Multiply (c) × 52	£———	= total paybill

Enter total absence days p.a.	———	(d)
Enter total number of working days p.a.	———	(e)
Divide [(d) × 100] by (e)	———	%(f) = absence rate
Multiply [(b)/5 × (d)]	£———	(g) = absence cost p.a.

Potential cost saving

Enter target reduction in total days absent p.a.	———	(h)
Divide (h) by (d)	———	(i)
Multiply (i) by (g)	£———	= total savings p.a.

Source: *Personnel and Profit*. London, IPM.

Using the above form for an organisation with 500 employees, average earnings of £250 per week, an average working year of 228 days per employee, and an absence level of 10 days per employee per year, we can calculate that the annual direct cost of absence is £250,000. A reduction in the absence level to 8 days would save £50,000 a year. This data could be produced on a disaggregated basis by establishments, departments or workgroups if necessary.

Monitoring absence

Whatever system(s) you eventually choose, somebody has to collect the information.

Monitoring absence levels is fundamental to absence control. When they decided to tackle absence, the first step Lewisham Council took was to establish what their absence problem was. Sometimes organisations don't even know what their absent rates are – as the Audit Commission discovered in its review of absence levels in London boroughs in 1991! We don't know the extent of this sort of ignorance country-wide because organisations that respond to absence questionnaires obviously do know what their levels are and therefore provide a biased sample.

But we do know that according to the Industrial Relations Services (1994) survey:

☐ the vast majority of organisations that do keep records do so on computer

☐ most recording is monthly (81 per cent of respondents to the IRS survey), followed by weekly (29 per cent) and quarterly (25 per cent)

☐ personnel departments and/or line managers are usually responsible for monitoring absence

☐ absence figures are broken down typically by department (84 per cent), broad occupational classification (eg manual/non-manual) (36 per cent), narrow occupational classification (32 per cent), and whether the absence was short- or long-term (36 per cent).

The more recent CBI survey (1997) casts further light on monitoring practice but includes a much higher proportion of small employers (nearly a third of respondents employ fewer than 100 people) which tends to bias the results. That survey concluded that only 18 per cent of organisations used computer recording alone, a further 51 per cent using both computer and manual recording. The same survey finds that in 73 per cent of organisations monitoring was the responsibility of personnel and/or line managers. (In practically all the remaining cases, senior managers carried out monitoring. There is an 'other' category but it is not clear what it covers – perhaps the occupational health or wages departments, or team leaders.) Interestingly, the CBI analysis suggests that absence is lower in terms of average days lost when senior managers (7.9 days) or line managers (8.0 days) have the responsibility for monitoring, than when personnel have it (9.1 days)!

Some cynical personnel professionals might wonder whether line managers are recording the information accurately. Nonetheless, it clearly makes sense to give the leading role in monitoring absence levels to the line. Not only are line managers likely to know the particular circumstances of each individual employee they manage, but they are also increasingly responsible for implementing the absence policies. More crucially, the line manager is often the contact point for employees who call in sick. Normally, sickness policies require employees to contact their line managers as early as possible on the first day of sickness, and to keep him or her informed on a regular basis if more than one day is taken.

Computerisation of itself does not reduce absence, and nor would you expect it to. Its contribution is indirect but nevertheless important. Computers help enormously with the collection, analysis and dissemination of absence statistics which are the basic building-blocks of successful absence management. It might be worth bearing in mind, however, that computerising records could initially seem to increase absence levels! Lewisham Council points out that in their experience better recording can result in a temporary increase in the absence level figure, which they say is a good sign – it means that levels are being more accurately recorded.

Benchmarking your organisation

All three of our case-studies at some point have looked at absence rates in other organisations as a pointer to assessing the degree to which they had an absence problem. This merely extends the concept of benchmarking performance, so common in other areas of organisation activity, to the issue of absence. Benchmarking is important because it tells you how well your organisation is performing against competitors and the world at large, highlighting areas for improvement, and helping to set performance standards.

Until fairly recently published information on absence rates for benchmarking purposes was difficult to find. Indeed, as late as 1993 the results of the CBI's (1987) survey were still quoted as the major source of absence levels data in the United Kingdom.

The gap was filled by occasional one-off surveys, as it still is to an extent, prepared by management consultancies and commentators such as Industrial Relations Services. But these often suffer from comparatively small sample sizes and/or a bias towards organisations likely to have the most sophisticated personnel policies.

Since 1993, both the CBI and the Industrial Society have published regular reports providing the latest data for benchmarking purposes. Both are surveys of employers.[1] The information in the surveys includes the overall absence rate, and breakdowns by region, sector, and organisation size. The Industrial Society also publishes data on absence by occupation.

One other important point to note from these data is that organisations which are smaller in terms of employee numbers have lower rates of absence than larger organisations. Because they tend to dominate the samples – 60 per cent of the CBI's respondents employed fewer than 500 people – larger organisations need to be aware that when comparing themselves to overall averages, or looking at the policies they have in relation to usage generally, they are probably not comparing like with like. As it is, both the CBI and Industrial Society surveys show that the smallest employers, under 500 employees, have below-average absence rates. Both sets of data also suggest that the highest rates apply in organisations of one to two or two-and-a-half thousand people – above that number rates fall again, even though they remain above average.

Secondly, at a disaggregated level some of the data from these sources can be very volatile over time. For example, comparing the CBI regional and industrial data for the last few years shows considerable movement in the rank order of the best and worst performers. Often this results from the very low sample sizes in some sectors and regions which can distort the results from year to year. You can have reasonable confidence in the broader figures, and in the more general occupational and industrial data. Otherwise it would be sensible to look at benchmarking data over a period of years to check whether there has been a lot of volatility and to decide how much faith you should attach to them.

Let us look now at what the data tell us. Overall, according to the CBI, in 1996 the average employee took 8.4 days off sick – an absence rate of 3.7 per cent – somewhat above the Industrial Society's rate of 3.59 per cent (approximately 8 days a year). The disaggregated figures show considerable variation.

By region, the CBI found that Northern Ireland had the worst absence record for manual workers (6.9 per cent) and southern England the best (2.9 per cent); and that for non-manual workers, the south-west was worst (4.8 per cent) and the north best (1.7 per cent).

By occupation, manual workers tend to have higher absence rates than non-manuals, and part-time manual workers higher rates than full-time manuals. The occupational relationship is confirmed by the Industrial Society figures, which show managers to have the lowest absence rates (1.33 per cent), followed by non-manual staff (2.76 per cent) and manuals (4.73 per cent). However, the Industrial Society found that for those companies that could give a figure, absence rates for full- and part-timers were roughly the same at just under 3 per cent.

Further occupational information can also be found in the quarterly *Labour Force Survey* (LFS), which collects data from households on a range of subjects including absence rates. The information is therefore based on responses from employees. The overall absence rate as at summer 1996 was 3.9 per cent according to this source – very close to the CBI figure. It shows absence lowest in professional occupations (about $2\frac{1}{2}$ per cent) and highest for plant and machine operators (5 per cent).

Only the Industrial Society collects data by gender, and this confirms other research that the absence rates of women are higher than those of men (3.09 per cent and 2.52 per cent, respectively). The Society advises that these figures be used only for general guidance because of the low sample size; they should certainly not be used as an excuse for discriminatory practices.

Absence by sector shows, as might be expected, absence rates lower in typical white-collar-type industries. In general terms the Industrial Society puts manufacturing (2.95 per cent) above financial services (2.62 per cent), but services buck the trend by having the highest absence rate in the private sector – 3.98 per cent. The overall highest rate (4.87 per cent) applies in the public/voluntary sector. The CBI data confirm this picture. According to them, the absence rate in the public sector was 4.5 per cent against 3.2 per cent in the private sector – indeed, the public sector exceeded the private sector rate irrespective of broad industrial classification or whether employees were full- or part-time. In fact, in the CBI's list of 22 industry sectors, public sector organisations have the four worst absence rates.

The *Labour Force Survey* more or less confirms this picture: employees in public administration and manufacturing are likely to have an higher absence rate (about $4\frac{1}{4}$ per cent) than in other major sectors; agriculture and fishing has the actual highest rate at over 5 per cent. The LFS also confirms the perhaps unexpected finding of the CBI survey that construction has one of the lowest rates of sickness absence (1.8 per cent according to the CBI, just over 3 per cent according to the LFS).

The CBI and Industrial Society are important sources of general information on absence levels. But you might want something less general and more specific to your needs – such as absence levels in your locality or sector, or for particular occupations. Options for gathering this kind of information include setting up a club of employers who agree to provide their absence rates, or using, say, an existing pay club survey to gather absence details. Another possibility is to seek the help of local employer bodies, such as Chambers of Commerce, or your own industry body, both of whom may already be collecting absence data.

When you have found benchmarking data that meets your needs, remember that your target should not be just to get your absence rate to the average. CBI data gives absence rates by average and quartile. It shows that in every sector some employers do substantially better than the average. In government agencies – the sector with the worst absence rate according to the CBI – the average number of days lost per employee per year was 10.6, but the best agencies lost only four days – well below the national average for all industries.

Getting to the average might be your immediate objective, but being amongst the best 25 per cent makes a better longer-term aim and will help to keep managing absence firmly on your organisation's agenda.

Conclusion

This chapter stresses the importance of measuring, monitoring and benchmarking data. Together they set the framework for managing absence. *Measuring* helps you understand the nature of your absenteeism; *monitoring* ensures that you have up-to-date information on where absence rates are going and is the foundation (as we shall see in Chapter 3) of many absence control policies; *benchmarking* means you know where you stand against comparators, and sets aims and objectives for your absence management programme. Another ingredient in effective policy design is *understanding* the causes of absence and their relevance to explaining absence in your organisation. We look at causes in the next chapter.

References

[1]The APAC survey carried by the Management Consultancy Group is a regular and useful source of general personnel information including absence. The information is available to participants only.

2

THE CAUSES OF ABSENCE

Any effective programme of absence control needs to start by analysing the causes of absence in order to devise the appropriate policies. As will be discussed further Chapter 5, an organisation's absence records will provide some guidance on the reasons given, days lost, frequency and overall patterns by department, grade, occupational group or location. It should be recognised, however, that any analysis of the reasons given for absence will suffer from certain limitations. Quite evidently, the reason given for short-term, self-certificated absence may or may not reflect the real underlying causes. It may therefore be worth carrying out a survey of the opinions of managers and supervisors and, if felt appropriate, employees themselves, about the causes.

The purpose of this chapter is to provide a summary of the main causes of absence identified by the research. The chapter emphasises that the causes of absence in any given organisation are unlikely, in most circumstances, to be explained by any single factor. Attempts by researchers to identify major single explanations of absence have been unsuccessful, and current thinking sees its causes in terms of multiple factors, the influence of which vary according to the organisational context. The chapter groups the causes into three categories: the influence of the personal characteristics of employees themselves; the influence of the organisation's policies and practices, or lack of them; and the influence of factors external to the organisation. Where further investigation – such as a survey of managers or supervisors – is under consideration, the absence described in the chapters should be assessed and those considered relevant to the specific organisational context should be explored further in the investigation.

Single-factor explanations of absence

Up to the late 1970s, much of the research into absence focused on trying to find a single factor to explain it. By implication, if the single factor causing absence from work could be identified, employers could tackle it through the implementation of the appropriate policies. According to Nicholson (1977), research had identified three main categories of causes of absence:

☐ pain avoidance
☐ adjustment to work
☐ economic decision-making by employees.

Pain avoidance

The major cause of absence here is job dissatisfaction, and the resultant form of absence is marked by its frequency. In essence, employees who are dissatisfied with their jobs seek to avoid the resulting psychological 'pain' or tensions of this by staying away from their jobs more often. We now know, however, that job dissatisfaction cannot be seen as the single cause of absenteeism but is certainly one of a number of factors in the work situation that influence absenteeism.

Adjustment to work

The main thrust of this explanation is that absence is the result of the way employees adapt or adjust to the situation found in a new workplace. One way of looking at absence is to view it as part of the socialisation process by which an individual adopts the absence norms and culture which he or she finds in an unfamiliar workplace. New employees observe the absence behaviour of their colleagues and its consequences from the response of management. Where there appears to be tolerance of absenteeism involving little action from management, new employees tend to conform by adopting the absence norms of their work group. Though these ideas are not new and were first put forward over 40 years ago (Hill and Trist, 1953; 1955), there has been a recent revival in interest in absence cultures at the level of the work group, and we shall be returning to them later in this chapter.

Another 'adjustment to work' perspective sees absence in terms of an employee's response to both the intrinsic and extrinsic rewards found in the workplace, and is associated with equity and exchange theory (Rhodes and Steers, 1990). In essence, this perspective argues that individuals expect a fair exchange between what they bring to their job in terms of their inputs of skills, knowledge, commitment and so on and the rewards or outcomes that they get out of it. These rewards may relate to intrinsic factors, such as job satisfaction, or extrinsic factors, such as pay and benefits. If individuals feel that there is some imbalance between their inputs and the outcomes, there is internal tension which they will seek to reduce. In this way, when individuals feel that either the intrinsic or extrinsic rewards fall short of their expectations, they will reduce the tension they may feel by putting less into the job. One possible response is to give the employer less of their time by going absent.

For management these ideas have several implications. First, if absence is seen by employees to be tolerated by management and carrying few consequences, employees are likely to adjust their absence behaviour accordingly. Moreover, employees expect fair rewards for their efforts. So, both job satisfaction and the provision of pay and benefits perceived as fair need to form part of any absence control strategy.

Economic decision-making by employees

This group of ideas sees absence as the result of rational decisions made by employees on the basis of their assessment of the costs and benefits associated with absence. Where absence is associated with a cost (such as loss of pay), an individual may nevertheless go absent because he or she values the alternative (such as a day off) more. A fine summer's day may be too good to miss by going in to work! Such theories do not, however, explain why one employee may feel sufficient commitment to go in to work, while another may stay away, but there has been research to support the view that the provision of occupational sick pay which either cushions or eliminates the economic cost of absence has led to higher levels of absenteeism – and this is a topic to which we shall return.

Integrated multiple-factor explanations of absence

More recent research has tended to emphasise the complex nature of the factors influencing absence and is associated in particular with the ideas of Nicholson (1977), Steers and Rhodes (1978; 1984) and Rhodes and Steers (1990). The implication of much of the earlier research was that absence was avoidable as long as its cause could be pinned down and the appropriate policies applied. Yet this did not explain how one employee might have a good attendance record while another might have a poor one. Explanations of absence behaviour needed instead, it was argued, to take into account variations in the personal characteristics, attitudes, values and backgrounds of individuals. Moreover, otherwise-motivated employees sometimes experienced constraints in their ability to attend. People did become genuinely ill and also got into domestic difficulties from time to time which prevented their attendance. As well as to enquire into why employees go absent, it was argued that it was equally pertinent to consider what factors influenced their attendance and what factors might prevent it. More recent explanations of absence thus take into account both absence and its converse, attendance.

One approach which takes into account factors influencing both absence and attendance is put forward by Nicholson (1977) and is illustrated in Figure 1. Nicholson starts from the not unreasonable assumption that attendance is normal behaviour, arguing that 'most people, most of the time, are on "automatic pilot" to attend regularly, and that the search for the causes of absence is a search for those factors that disturb the regularity of attendance' (ibid, p.242). Whether they will actually attend in a given set of circumstances depends on a number of variables. The key variables are those that affect 'attachment and attendance motivation', each of which is influenced by a 'contextual factor'. First, the personal characteristics of individuals, such as age or gender, influence

Figure 1

NICHOLSON'S MODEL OF ATTENDANCE MOTIVATION

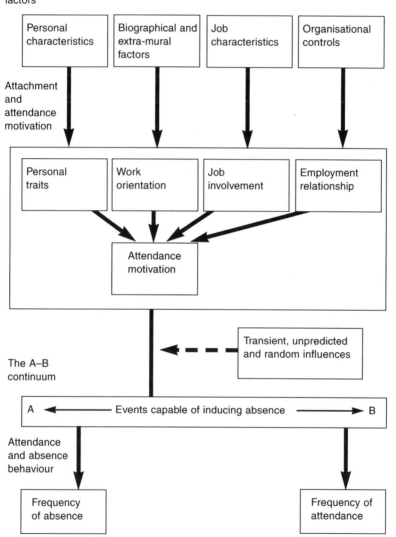

Source: Nigel Nicholson (1977), 'Absence Behavior and Attendance Motivation: A Conceptual Synthesis', *Journal of Management Studies, 14*(13), p.251. Copyright © Basil Blackwell Ltd.

absence. For example, older workers are likely to take more time off through sickness. Secondly, orientations or attitudes to work differ according to occupational experience and background, reflected, for example, in higher levels of absence amongst manual than non-manual workers. Thirdly, the nature of jobs and the opportunities they provide for satisfaction and involvement vary, again reflected in the differences between manual and non-manual worker absence. A fourth influence arises out of the rules of the workplace which may be either strict or lenient on absence. A final influence is referred to as 'random' and refers to domestic or travel difficulties which may affect the ability to attend.

The result is an absence continuum, ranging from unavoidable influences (A) which impact on frequency of absence to avoidable influences (B) impacting on frequency of attendance. Nicholson argues that absence control policies should be aimed at tackling the avoidable influences, recognising that these will vary between individuals and work settings. For example, a minor ailment experienced by an older worker performing heavy manual work may be more likely to result in an absence than the same ailment experienced by a younger worker performing light office work, and if an organisation seeks to set targets for achievement, these differences need to be recognised. The model provides a useful focus on a range of factors influencing attendance and non-attendance which absence management policies need to address, with an emphasis on those absences which may be seen as 'avoidable' in a given organisational context. These will be explored in more detail later in the chapter.

Steers and Rhodes' (1978) 'process model of employee attendance' starts from the characteristics of the job, which in turn influence job satisfaction and motivation to attend. Like Nicholson, these authors also recognise that job satisfaction and motivation are in turn affected by personal characteristics which influence attendance – for example, that older age affects the likelihood of sickness, and that higher educational attainments are more likely to lead to the pursuit of a career or profession with which lower absence levels are associated.

The model also incorporates the idea of 'pressures to attend'. In times of economic uncertainty, for example, fear of losing

Figure 2

RHODES AND STEERS' MODEL OF EMPLOYEE ATTENDANCE

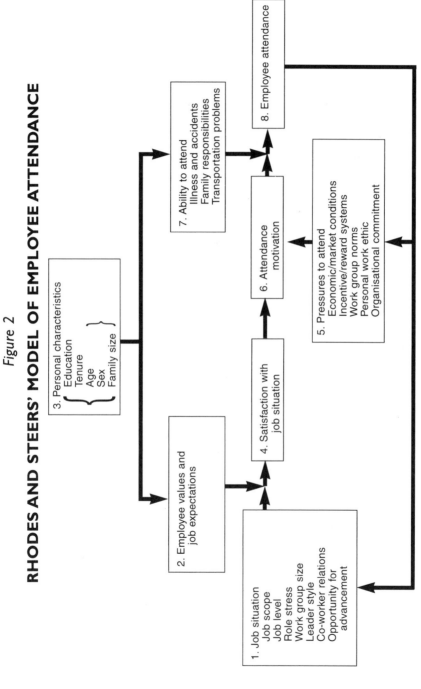

Source: Rhodes and Steers, 1990, p.46.

one's job may result in pressures not to be absent. Work group or peer pressures may act either to encourage absence or attendance, according to the prevailing cultural norms. Loss of pay or an attendance bonus may also act to discourage absence. Finally, like Nicholson's, the model recognises the role of ability to attend. Circumstances arise, even for the most highly motivated employee, in which attendance is not possible. Genuine illness is one obvious example, as are family responsibilities and travel difficulties. Ability to attend is also influenced by the employee's personal circumstances. For example, size of family is likely to increase constraints on ability to attend, as is distance from home to work or the complexity of the journey undertaken. Absence patterns thus vary between individuals according to the particular influences on their behaviour. From a management perspective, the model therefore stresses the importance of understanding the prevailing influences on absence for each group of employees and applying the appropriate policies.

Subsequently, Rhodes and Steers (1990) developed what they term a 'diagnostic model of employee attendance' for use by managers in understanding absence in their organisations. This is illustrated in Figure 3. It recognises three key influences on attendance motivation.

First, organisational practices need to set out clear attendance standards and procedures, pay due attention to work design, involve recruitment and selection practices that screen for past absence behaviour, and incorporate the communication of clear attendance standards to staff. Second, the importance of absence cultures should be recognised. In the absence of appropriate control policies, employee behaviours are likely to reflect the norms of the work group, which may either stress attendance or encourage absence. In addition to clear attendance standards, absence cultures can be influenced by attention to work design and the establishment of self-managing teams with highly interdependent roles. The third area of influence is on employee attitudes, values and goals which are in turn strongly influenced by the kinds of organisational practices and cultures considered above.

The diagnostic model also incorporates factors which may act as barriers to attendance – such as illness, family responsi-

Figure 3

A DIAGNOSTIC MODEL OF EMPLOYEE ATTENDANCE

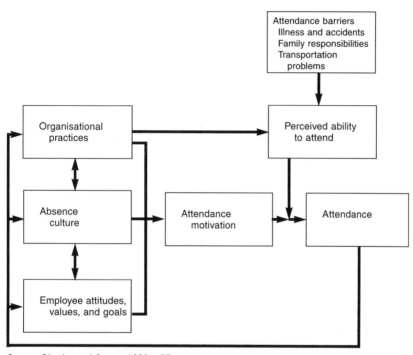

Source: Rhodes and Steers, 1990, p.57.

bilities and travel problems – but which may also be influenced by organisational policies. While organisations are unlikely to want genuinely sick employees to come to work, company health-care programmes, occupational health services and employee-assistance programmes can all help to create a healthier workforce. Various approaches are available to reduce absence arising out of family responsibilities: for example, child-care facilities, special leave or flexibility to allow occasional working from home. Travel difficulties may be alleviated through the provision of company bus services, car pooling or other arrangements.

Now that we have considered a number of models, the remainder of the chapter will examine in more detail the various factors included in these models and assess their significance as potential causes of absence. The various factors will be scrutinised under three headings: first, differences in absence due to the personal characteristics of individuals; second, factors within the direct influence of organisations; and third, factors external to the workplace.

The influence of personal characteristics on absence

The personal characteristics identified by Rhodes and Steers (1990) and Huczynski and Fitzpatrick (1989) are:

- length of service
- age
- gender
- personality
- employee attitudes, values and expectations
- past absence behaviour.

Length of service

It might be expected that absence would decrease with length of service as employees form ties of loyalty with the organisation and, where internal labour market hierarchies operate, they achieve promotion to higher grade or status positions by virtue of service. The research findings provide some support for a link between longer service and lower absence, but in practice the linkage is complicated by other factors that can also affect absence levels (Huczynski and Fitzpatrick,1989). For example, many organisations provide occupational sick pay only after certain periods of service, and some increase entitlement with service. As we have noted and will return to again, there is evidence linking the payment of sick pay with higher absence levels, since the costs of absence to the individual become less where sick pay is provided. Absence levels could rise with service for this reason. Also, length of service is associated with age, which in turn has characteristic influences on absence as we shall see shortly. In conclusion, then, length of service may be one factor that influences absence levels, but it is not a decisive one.

Age

There is general agreement from the research that younger people tend to have more frequent short spells of absence whereas older people have fewer short spells but are absent longer in each spell, especially after the age of 50 (*ibid*,1989). Age is, therefore, an important factor in absence, especially in the pattern of absence that comprises the frequent short spell which is often seen as more disruptive.

Gender

The general pattern which emerges from statistics on absence is that females have higher rates than males. However, as with the length of service variable discussed above, the underlying explanation for this may not lie in the gender difference *per se*, but rather in other variables that affect male and female roles, both at work and in the wider society. By way of example, there is evidence that female absence falls as the age of dependent children rises (*ibid*,1989), indicating that some female absence results from a woman's role as carer in the family, involving the consequent need to take time off to look after sick children or elderly relatives. The role of family responsibilities has been recognised as a constraint on the ability of individuals to attend work in various studies of the causes of absence, and will be reviewed again in a later section on external influences. In addition, explanations of female absence patterns can also be found that relate to the occupational structure, since a higher proportion of females than males occupies lower occupational positions, and a lower proportion reaches senior roles with which lower absence rates may be associated as a result of different career values and expectations. There is no evidence, for example, that where women occupy senior positions their absence levels are not any higher than those of men in equivalent roles (*ibid*,1989). This raises some questions. Given that family responsibilities may be a cause of female absence, the answer may lie in the ability of women in higher-paid roles to afford domestic assistance. Clearly, influence of gender on absence is complex, and gender of itself may be a less important explanation for absence than other independent variables which affect women's work and women's roles in the wider society.

Personality

Absence research has identified that a relatively high proportion of absence within a given workforce can be attributed to a relatively small proportion of the total workforce. This is, of course, a well known phenomenon sometimes known as the '80/20 rule' and is attributed to the Italian economist Vilfredo Pareto. In the case of absence, it has been found, for example, that up to half of all absence can be accounted for by as little as 5 to 10 per cent of the workforce (ibid, 1989). Absence research has endeavoured to investigate this phenomenon by attempting to identify personality factors that might lead an individual to become 'absence prone'. The main conclusion as a result of personality testing is that those who demonstrate personality characteristics of anxiety and emotional instability are more likely to be absent than those who are more introverted and emotionally stable (ibid, 1989). Stress is also a factor in absence, and people's abilities to cope with it vary according to personality characteristics – a key one being what is known as the 'locus of control'. This personality attribute sees people as broadly divided into two personality types: 'internals' who perceive themselves as having a high degree of control over factors influencing their lives, and 'externals' who see themselves as the pawns of fate, their lives largely directed by external forces over which they have little or no control. Research has shown that 'internals' feel better able to take control of and directly influence stressful situations, in comparison with 'externals' who are more likely to experience greater stress because of their feeling of inability to control it. 'Externals' are also more likely to experience poorer health and higher absence rates than 'internals' (Robbins, 1993). It may be concluded that personality differences do influence absence levels – but interesting though all this is, for all practical purposes there is not much that organisations can do about it!

Employee attitudes, values and expectations

This is a complex issue that has attracted much attention on the part of industrial sociologists and psychologists over many years, and anything approaching a full discussion is beyond the scope of the present text. In any event, there is no general agreement and the issue is one of considerable debate. Clearly, attitudes, values and expectations will in part be influenced outside the workplace as a result of family, education, community, class and other influences in people's upbringings. They will also be influenced by the experience of work generally, and for some people activities other than work will be more central to their life goals. Where family responsibilities, hobbies or other non-work interests take precedence, it might reasonably be expected that this will be conducive to higher absence (Rhodes and Steers, 1990). At the same time, attitudes can change – for example, as a result of experience in an organisational setting. For our purposes we can assume that absence behaviour will in part result from attitudes, values and behaviour personal to individuals, formed outside the workplace, but also recognise that attitudes may either change or be reinforced by the prevailing culture of the organisation and the controls operated by management. This is a topic to which we shall return in this chapter and elsewhere in this book.

Past absence behaviour

Research indicates that one of the strongest indicators of future absence behaviour is past absence behaviour and, moreover, that absence frequency has been found to be a stronger predictor than total number of days lost (Rhodes and Steers, 1990; Huczynski and Fitzpatrick, 1989). Whatever the reasons, this finding has clear implications for the screening process at recruitment – and this is a matter to which we shall return in the next chapter.

The influence of the organisational context

The influence of the organisational context as a cause of absence may be seen from four distinct perspectives:

☐ work design
☐ other job-related factors
☐ work group norms and cultures
☐ organisational policies and practices in relation to absence.

The components of each of these perspectives will be examined in turn in this section.

Work design

There has for many years been considerable discussion about the impact of the design of jobs on employee attitudes and behaviours, in terms of motivation, commitment, quality of work and so on, and some of this discussion has extended to absenteeism. The 'scientific management' approach to the design of work has tended to predominate in the twentieth century and is based on the principles of a high degree of division of labour and specialisation, with the general result that many work roles consist mainly of simple, fragmented, routine and repetitive tasks. Such ideas are popularly associated with the 'scientific management' approach advocated by the American engineer F.W. Taylor (1911) and also reflect the predominant influence of people with engineering training in the design of jobs in modern organisations. The stereotyped image is of the production line worker, but there is a view that the division of labour, task specialisation and deskilling have gone far beyond this to affect most jobs in some way (Braverman, 1974). Offices are thus seen as 'white-collar factories', and even management jobs have become functionally specialised to the extent that one department has little idea of what goes on in another. The advantages of such an approach are usually expressed in terms of the efficiency gains of specialisation. By implication, each individual is only capable of assimilating and deploying a limited range of expertise in a given field, and by focusing on this field alone he or she becomes proficient. The disadvantages of such an approach have long been recognised. Where it has been carried to extremes, the results have been boredom, apathy and minimal commitment to the job and the organisation. More recently, some wider ramifications have also been recognised. Task specialisation, leading to a narrow and inflexible skills base within the workforce, has done little to equip people to adapt to rapid changes in the environment, with the result that they are likely to resist changes that threaten the narrow skills base from which they draw their livelihood. Moreover, it has done little to encourage learning as the starting-point for adapting to rapid change. Given also the recognition of quality as a key factor in competitiveness, traditional work fragmentation has tended to diffuse responsibility for quality, the effects of which were plain to see until the recent growth of interest in this topic.

It is now pertinent to enquire into the potential effects of traditional approaches to work design on absence. Common sense would suggest that employees who experience routine and repetitive work, with low levels of autonomy, responsibility and decision-making, are likely to experience minimal commitment to their jobs and may be more likely to take time off. Rhodes and Steers (1990) conclude from their review of the research into the general effects of scientific management on job design that 'negative outcomes include lower job satisfaction, lower motivation and higher absenteeism'. They go on to argue, on the basis of a review of absence studies carried in the mid- to late 1980s, that investigations into 'the relationship between job satisfaction dimensions and absenteeism have uniformly found that the strongest relationship exists between work satisfaction and [low] absence frequency'. They conclude that lack of job involvement is particularly closely concerned with absence frequency. In a similar vein, Huczynski and Fitzpatrick (1989) conclude that 'a great deal of research associates high levels of task repetitiveness with low job satisfaction [which] in turn has been positively correlated with absence'. Surveys of managers' opinions about the causes of absence also tend to bear this out. One third of the managers in the Industrial Society's (1997) absence survey identified low morale and a boring job as major causes of absence, ranking these fourth in a league table after colds and 'flu, stress and personal problems, and domestic problems. The consensus of opinion thus appears to be that there is a relationship between routine, repetitive and fragmented tasks under traditional scientific management approaches to job design which are likely to lead to higher absence frequency. If this is so, it should be expected that initiatives to redesign jobs to reduce the routine, repetitive and fragmented nature of them ought to have the opposite effect – of lowering absence frequency – and this is a question to which we shall return in Chapter 4.

Other job-related factors

In addition to the important issue of job design, a number of other job-related factors have been identified by Huczynski and

Fitzpatrick (1989) as having an influence on absence, and they are briefly reviewed in this section.

Stress Against a background of downsizing and delayering and increased pressures on individuals to deliver high performance, it is now recognised that work-related stress can affect all levels in the organisational hierarchy. One government study, *Mental Health at Work* (1988), found evidence of growing minor psychiatric disorders at work and suggested that 40 per cent of absence from work through illness could be attributed to mental and emotional problems. Cary Cooper (in Huczynski and Fitzpatrick, 1989) has identified a number of causes of stress at work.

The first relates to the conditions in which a job is performed. Poor working conditions, physical dangers, even the distractions created in an open-planned office environment all cause stress. Research has shown that factories that have poor standards of housekeeping or poorly equipped or maintained machinery, or offices which are drably furnished, poorly lit or poorly heated, can have higher absence levels.

A second cause of stress is shiftwork, although its relationship to absence is not entirely clear. Warr and Yearta (1995) found that shift workers were more likely than others to be absent for sickness or injury. This was particularly marked amongst male shift workers on two-shift schedules or rotating three-shift cycles, but less so amongst females.

A third cause of stress has to do with work overload or underload (including repetitive work or periods of low activity causing boredom between periods of high activity). Studies have connected both work overload and underload with absence.

A fourth cause has to do with role ambiguity (lack of clarity about what is expected) and role conflict (where the expectations are clear, but they conflict with each other). Role conflict can also arise where there is conflict between work demands and other non-work roles, such as the family. Research has shown that role ambiguity and role conflict are both causes of stress, higher absence and serious illness.

A fifth factor relates to career development. There are two aspects here: overpromotion, associated with difficulties in coping, and underpromotion, associated with feelings of lack of status or recognition and stifled career ambitions.

Other factors include poor relationships at work, lack of consultation and little participation in decision-making. Stress is increasingly being recognised as a significant cause of workplace absence, and in the opinion of managers who responded to the Industrial Society's (1997) survey on absence it was the second most important cause of time lost. The issues raised in this section are wide-reaching, encompassing working conditions, patterns of working hours, workloads, career and promotional prospects and workplace relationships, not to mention stress caused by factors outside the workplace, and serve to indicate just how broad comprehensive absence control programmes may have to be.

Frequency of job moves As has long been recognised, work fulfils social needs for many people, involving opportunities to form ties of loyalty with work colleagues. There is some evidence that where employees are required to move frequently within their workplaces to meet the needs of flexibility or where systems of job rotation are in place, the negative effect of this on people's social needs can result in higher absence.

Leadership style A number of studies have identified links between the style of first line supervisors and absence behaviour in work groups. For example, employees who feel more able to discuss their problems with their supervisor have been found to go absent less than those who felt unable to do so.

Organisation and work group size National surveys of absence have consistently shown that total days lost through absence rise fairly consistently with the total number of people employed. So, for example, the CBI (1997) found absence rates of under 3 per cent in organisations of less than 100 employees, rising to around 4 per cent in organisations employing 1,000 or more people. The reasons for this are not entirely clear, but are likely to be bound up with the process of bureaucratisation and the tendency for work group sizes to become larger and work roles to become more specialised in bigger organisations. In smaller organisations, individuals' roles are likely to be more visible and multiskilled and less easily covered during absence, making the impact of their absence more disruptive and more noticeable to colleagues and management. Such visibility becomes less in larger organisations, which may have more scope to provide cover and where absences become less noticeable within the multiple layers of supervision and management. Recent moves towards delayering, decentralisation to strategic business units, empowerment and multi-tasking within larger enterprises may have the effect of reducing the influence of organisation size on absence behaviour, but this has yet to be substantiated by research evidence.

Work group norms and cultures

The influence of work group norms on behaviour has been recognised since the famous Hawthorne experiments of the 1920s and 1930s (Roethlisberger and Dickson, 1939). We noted earlier, in our consideration of the 'adjustment to work' models of absence behaviour, that absence levels may be associated with the process of both formal and informal organisational socialisation. The formal process of socialisation involves the communication of the organisation's rules and standards of conduct, reinforced (or not, as the case may be) by the subsequent behaviour of those authorised to enforce them. People fairly quickly get to understand whether the rules operate in practice or whether they are just part of management rhetoric and can effectively be ignored. Informal socialisation occurs where new employees, on arrival within their work group, fairly quickly learn what behaviour is appropriate. In the case of absence, they learn by observation what the absence behaviours of the group are and their consequences in terms of any action taken by superiors. Because most people want to be accepted by the group of which they are a part, they tend to conform to the established norms: groups will often bring a range of pressures to bear to ensure that behavioural norms are enforced. Norms can be of various types, but probably the most common relate to standards of performance, of which absence is a part. Norms arise, therefore, out of the formal rules established by management and the rigour with which management enforces them on the one hand, and the informal rules established by work groups on the other – the latter being strongly influenced by the former. Formal and informal norms are therefore closely interrelated.

A powerful source of norms is 'custom and practice': an informal process of joint accommodation between managers, supervisors and work groups about what behaviour will be accepted. Custom and practice has its roots in the history of management and work group relationships in a given workplace; it sets precedents and establishes powerful expectations about what behaviours are acceptable and what disciplinary sanctions will be applied when acceptable norms of behaviour are transgressed. The 'rules' generated by custom and practice form precedents based on the past action taken by management in given situations and are reinforced by notions of fairness and equity. Where certain transgressions (such as absence) have been overlooked in the past, there will be powerful expectations on the part of the work group that they will also be overlooked in the future on grounds of consistency and fairness. The opposite will also be true: there will be expectations within the work group that past penalties for given offences will also be applied in the future. Custom and practice is the outcome of the relative bargaining power of management to enforce sanctions and the work group to resist them. This process may either be formal, reinforced by trade union action in support of their members in disciplinary situations, or informal, part of the daily process of accommodation and 'give and take' between supervisors and work groups in order to maintain morale and good will.

It will be evident from the foregoing discussion that not just the words but also the actions of managements have an important influence on establishing acceptable norms of behaviour. Where certain types of absence (such as the odd day off) or indeed absence in general have tended to be overlooked in the past, there will strong expectations that it will continue to be so in the future. Changing this situation requires managements to broadcast clear and powerful signals that there is to be a break with the past.

So far, absence culture has been seen as part of a process of negotiated agreement between management and work groups in which the enforcement of rules plays a significant role in establishing work group norms and expectations. There can be little doubt that organisational policies and practices, whether established unilaterally by management or jointly agreed with trade unions, are important influences on absence – and we shall return to this theme in the next chapter. Another perspective on absence culture has also emerged more recently: the discipline of peer pressure associated with the idea of self-managing teams and its potential for absence reduction – and this is a theme to which we shall also be returning.

Organisational practices and policies

Organisational policies and practices regarding attendance and absence are conventionally viewed in the literature on absence management as part of the 'cure' for absenteeism, not its cause. In this respect, the present publication is no different, and a range of policies for absence reduction is examined in Chapter 3. However, it would also be sensible to look at current policies as part of the cause of absence, since cause and effect are closely interrelated. This section of the chapter has been concerned with the organisational context of absence. By implication, the causes of absence considered here result from decisions consciously or unconsciously made by managements and therefore lie within their power to alter. So if the research suggests that traditional, fragmented job roles involving routine and repetitive tasks, the minimum of variety and a lack opportunities to learn new skills tend to encourage higher absence levels, it is open to managements to think up alternative ways of organising tasks to be undertaken by flexible, self-managing teams which the research suggests tend to encourage higher attendance levels. If lack of any clear framework of rules, or the consistent application of any framework of rules established, has encouraged cultural norms that tolerate certain levels of absence, the responsibility for changing this position lies entirely within the remit of an organisation's management.

It is not necessary here to extend this discussion further, for a more comprehensive review of the options available for absence control makes up much of the next chapter, but suffice it to note that causes and consequences are closely interrelated.

It is worth concluding this section by focusing on one aspect of organisational policies that has received some attention in the research: the links between an organisation's sick pay policies and levels of absence. The general conclusion from Britain and other countries is that where more generous sickness benefits are provided, absence levels tend to rise. This has been found to be so either where the costs of sickness benefit are met mainly by the state (as in Germany) or where they are met through employers' occupational sick pay schemes, as in Britain or the United States (Huczynksi and Fitzpatrick, 1989). Research has also shown that employees in organisations not covered by occupational sick pay – such as those with short service or on temporary contracts – have lower levels of absence than employees who are covered by such schemes (ibid). A related issue is the emergence of cultural expectations to the effect that a certain amount of paid sick leave is an 'entitlement' to be taken, rather like paid holiday entitlement. This possibility was considered by over a third of the respondents to the CBI's (1997) absence survey to be a significant cause of manual worker absence. It is not being suggested here that organisations should do away with sick pay because it encourages absence, but rather that the management of absence should be subject to closer control so that potential abuses are minimised. This is a topic to which we shall also return.

The influence of external factors on absence

In this section of the chapter, we consider a range of potential causes of absence that emanate mainly from outside the workplace and may therefore lie outside the immediate control of managements – although there are certain initiatives available to help control even these external influences. The main external influences on absence, which were viewed by the models considered at the beginning of the chapter as restricting employees' 'ability to attend', are:

- economic and market conditions
- genuine illness and accidents
- travel and transport problems
- family responsibilities.

Each of these is considered in turn below.

Economic and market conditions

Research provides some evidence that employees' propensity to attend or take time off is related to their perceptions of the state of the job market. During times of economic boom, relatively lower levels of unemployment and plentiful job vacancies, people thus feel more secure in their jobs or more confident of their ability to find another one, and are more prepared to take time off. Conversely, in times of recession, higher unemployment and less job security, the reverse is true and absence levels tend to fall. Such behaviour may be more conspicious where absence levels form one of the criteria used for redundancy selection which, according to IRS (1995b), has increasingly become the case amongst employers in Britain. Partial support for the proposition that absence levels are affected by economic and market conditions can be found in the periodic national surveys of absence conducted by the leading management or employer organisations. The CBI, for example, found that national absence rates rose amid the economic boom of the later 1980s, but fell quite sharply in the recessionary conditions after 1991. Absence rates amongst all employees rose from 3.6 to 4 per cent between 1987 and 1991, fell back a little to around 3.5 per cent from 1992 to 1994, thereafter rising slightly with recovery (CBI, 1993; 1997).

However, if this hypothesis were to be fully consistent it might be expected that regions of the country experiencing higher levels of unemployment might generally experience lower levels of absence – but the data from surveys such as that of the CBI do not confirm this. In their 1997 survey, for example, the region with the highest absence rate for manual workers (Northern Ireland) was also the region with the highest level of unemployment, while Greater London had the second highest rate of manual worker absence but much lower levels of unemployment. Differences may in part be explained by variations in the occupational structure of a given region, particularly where male manuals (who tend to have higher levels of absence) make up a larger proportion of total employment in the region.

We may conclude, therefore, that organisations experience rises and falls in overall absence levels according to changes in economic and market conditions but such fluctuations do not appear to be particularly significant. As outlined in the Introduction to this book, much more significant are the differences in absence level between organisations in the same industry, differences which remain constant whatever the economic or market conditions in that industry. The actions pursued by management within an organisation seem to be more influential on absence levels than the impact of economic or market factors.

Genuine illness and accidents

The existence of genuine illness as a cause of absence seems obvious, yet it is sometimes neglected in writings on the subject which tend to imply that the problem of absenteeism can be solved totally through the application of the appropriate policies. Although it is impossible to be certain about the extent to which genuine illness features in total absence statistics, over 90 per cent of respondents to the CBI's (1997) absence survey considered that genuine illness was the major contributor to time lost, and it has been estimated that genuine illness accounts for between a half and two thirds of all absence (Huczynski and Fitzpatrick, 1989). Research has shown that sickness absence, especially amongst males, is age-related, an increase in absence levels occurring after the age of 40 and increasing more sharply after the age of 50 (Warr and Yearta, 1995).

We also noted earlier the potential contribution of stress, both work- and non-work-related, and it is estimated that this may account for up to 40 per cent of all sickness absence. The significance of stress has also featured in surveys of managers' opinions about the causes of absence. In the Industrial Society's (1997) survey, managers rated stress and emotional/personal problems as the second most significant cause of absence after colds and 'flu.

A further factor is alcohol-related absence which the DSS has estimated to account for 5 per cent of days lost through sickness absence per annum.

In all, therefore, genuine sickness absence must be seen as a major cause of days lost, but one which more and more organisations are seeking to tackle through the rapid rise in employee assistance programmes, counselling and other initiatives to promote better health awareness.

Travel and transport problems

A number of studies have shown that transport and travel difficulties can affect people's ability to attend work even if they are
motivated to do so. Associated factors include the length of the
journey to work, weather conditions, traffic congestion, and the
standard of public transport services. Studies have tended to
show that the longer the journey – especially if exacerbated by
bad weather or traffic congestion – the greater the likelihood
that people will give up or not even attempt it. Although these
factors may be seen as largely outside the control of employers,
they could be taken into account when making recruitment and
selection decisions, when making decisions about the location
of workplaces, or when contemplating the provision of transport services for employees where the final part of the journey
to a workplace is subject to poor public service provision.

Family responsibilities

We noted earlier that one factor that contributes to gender
differences in absence statistics relates to responsibilities for
the family – that elderly relatives may affect the ability of
women to attend work – and, no doubt, a proportion of male
absence can be attributed to this factor also. Research indicates
that women's absence rates increase with family size, but
decline as the age of dependent children increases. The overall
absence statistics for women show that absence rates also
decline as they get older (Huczynski and Fitzpatrick, 1989).
This provides fairly strong evidence in support of the view that
family responsibilities are a significant cause of absence.
Moreover, that view is supported by the opinions expressed by
managers in absence surveys. In the Industrial Society's (1997)
survey, more than half of the managers identified sickness in
the family, child-care problems and other domestic responsibilities as significant causes of absence, placing it third in a league
table of causes after colds and 'flu and stress/personal problems.
A similar view was taken by the managers responding to the
CBI's (1997) absence survey, nearly half of them rating family
responsibilities as a major cause of absence, second only to
genuine illness. Family responsibilities can, therefore, be a
significant cause of absence and can inspire employees otherwise properly motivated to respond by placing family needs over

pressures to attend work. This highlights the need to ensure that policies to reduce absence are appropriate to the cause. For example, family responsibilities are an aspect of absence which employers may seek to influence through flexible working time arrangements, crèches or other special leave arrangements.

Conclusions

As is evident from the information presented in this chapter, absence is a complex topic and its causes are many and varied. We have considered these causes under three broad headings: personal characteristics, organisational policies, and external factors which act to inhibit individuals' abilities to attend. While some of these influences may be outside the control of employers, it is possible to identify a host of causes of absence which can be tackled through the implementation of the appropriate policies. These causes in summary are:

- employee attitudes and expectations
- lack of appropriate organisational controls
- rigid and inflexible job design and lack of empowerment
- lack of opportunities for teamworking
- poor working conditions and environment
- work overload or underload
- frustrated career and promotion prospects
- interpersonal problems in the workplace
- ineffective screening at recruitment and selection
- stress, caused either within the workplace or outside it
- inappropriate management styles
- an organisational culture that fails to discourage absence
- lack of priority given to the promotion of workforce health and wellbeing
- failure to recognise the significance of domestic responsibilities and a lack of flexibility in employment policies.

The implementation of policies to tackle these issues is the subject of the next chapter.

3

ABSENCE CONTROL AND ATTENDANCE MANAGEMENT POLICIES

In Chapter 1 we looked at measuring, monitoring and benchmarking absence, and in Chapter 2 we considered the causes of absence. This chapter outlines the policy options that employers have for *controlling* absence. Because 'controlling absence' sounds negative – and evidence suggests that policies aimed purely at control can actually lead to higher absence by undermining employee commitment – managers nowadays increasingly look to *manage* attendance: that is, to create an environment in which employees are more likely to want to come to work than to stay at home. As we shall see, survey analysis suggests that this latter approach tends to be the most successful in reducing absence levels. With its emphasis on incentives, teamworking and employee involvement, managing absence approaches also seem closer to human resource philosophies than traditional personnel management attitudes.

What sort of policies?

The main objective of absence policies is really to encourage people to want to come to work when they would rather be at home (although no good employer sets out to pressurise the genuinely ill to return to work before they are well enough to do so). Incidences of absence therefore fall on a continuum running from genuine ill-health at one extreme, which demands one set of policies, to lack of motivation at the other, which requires totally different approaches. In between are any number of combinations of ill-health and motivation which policies must tackle.

Because it is a complex subject, there is no universal panacea to managing absence. There are, however, a whole raft of policies employers can choose from. The CBI lists 12 approaches, but others (eg Scott and Markham, 1982) have found up to 34 different policies. Not all of them were necessarily originally introduced to reduce absence, but that does seem to have been one by-product of their adoption. Policies to tackle absence follow six themes:

- involvement of line management
- rewards for good attendance, ie incentives
- formal and informal sanctions, ie penalties
- work redesign and flexible working
- supporting employees with family commitments
- occupational health programmes and promotions.

This chapter looks at policy options in relation to these themes.

But before looking at policies in more detail, we should emphasise again the importance of an absence management framework built around gathering information, disseminating it to managers (and others), and getting feedback about absence trends and how policies are operating. These were all the subject of Chapter 1.

The role of the line manager

In the line manager two important threads of successful absence management come together: the measurement and monitoring of absence figures and the implementation of absence policies. A feature of devolved organisations is the empowering of line managers to manage their staff, within guidelines prepared by the personnel department, but with a very hands-off personnel approach – at least until a stage where the disciplinary procedure is invoked. Our case-studies, and others reported elsewhere, emphasise the central role played by line managers in absence control.

At the basic level, line managers are increasingly the major players in the collection of absence statistics, which makes sense because they are usually the first contact-point for employees who report sick. They are also the interface between management and managed, the people charged with implementing policies at the lowest level. Lewisham Council's absence approach was based on cascading down objectives from a strategic (ie Council-wide) level to departments and then down to individuals via line managers and supervisors, 'all underpinned by the fundamental view that line managers were the people best placed to deal with absence issues'.

Their role included keeping accurate attendance records, making sure employees were aware of the policy on absence, and implementing the various stages of the absence management programme as they were triggered.

A similar approach exists at the Royal Mail, where the line managers are expected to make the decision whether to proceed through the stages of the absence management programme taking account of the circumstances and history of each individual concerned.

The common themes, therefore, are first: disseminating absence information back to line managers as frequently as possible (monthly seems most favoured) and in as disaggregated a form as necessary. Computerised systems have a valuable role in allowing managers to be informed the instant an employee crosses a 'trigger-point' into a different phase of the absence policy. Second: absence targets are set. Often these are set centrally, but at Lewisham the approach allowed departments to set their own targets, within the overall guidelines, so that they could progress at a pace suitable to their own environment. Achievement against target is publicised so that performance is clear to all employees – some organisations go as far as to publish absence league tables to generate an element of competition between managers.

Line managers also need encouragement and guidance. Organisations do find that line managers can prefer to let absence policies wither through lack of use, particularly if they think, as they often seem to, that 'if you're sick you're sick' and that is the end of the story, or that the policy is being less rigorously applied in some areas than others and that *senior managers are not themselves particularly committed to absence control.*

Lewisham found that in its social services department line managers were not implementing crucial aspects of the policy, such as carrying out return-to-work interviews or outlining to staff what constituted an acceptable level of absence. The answer was a combination of including implementation of the absence policy in line managers' personal performance objectives while helping them get over their particular aversion to carrying out return-to-work interviews by using a specially appointed personnel officer to assist at 100 pilot interviews.

Assistance also comes from preparing written guidance and/or using videos so that managers know what is expected of them. That sounds self-evident but IRS (1994) found that only 55 per cent of organisations in their survey had special written guidance for line managers on handling absence. And it needs quite an investment in training so that managers understand the reasons why people might stay away from work, how absence may be controlled, their responsibilities and options in controlling absence, and their role in counselling and offering assistance to employees.

Involving line managers in absence control requires a big investment in training. It is not a one-off investment. Absence policies often develop over time to match changing circumstances, so keeping managers fully equipped to deal with the demands placed on them is a continuing process.

Monitoring the sick employee

We said that line managers provide the interface with the bulk of employees and that organisations have increasingly devolved the day-to-day management of absence to them. A major feature of the line managers' role involves monitoring the sick employee. This takes two forms: keeping in touch with people while they are off sick, and interviewing them on their return.

Keeping in touch with the employee doesn't need to be done in an overbearing way: reasonably regular 'phone calls will do just to check how the employee is recovering and his or her likely date of return. It is important to talk to the employee direct, not to rely on talking to a member of the family (except in circumstances of hospitalisation, for example) or on reports from work colleagues along the lines of 'I saw old Joe on Saturday and he says he'll be off another three weeks.' Some companies (eg Nissan) carry out home visits. These can take two guises: first, where the employee is away on long-term sick leave and where visits have a distinct welfare element to them; and second, in cases where management have reason to believe an employee is abusing the system. Such visits can throw up interesting results. After fruitlessly knocking on the door of an absent employee, one line manager/personnel officer team was told by a neighbour that they were wasting their time as 'He always works on his market stall on Mondays.' That particular employee is no longer with the company, his case not helped by his claiming absence due to a bad back. Other cases include employees running taxi firms or working in pubs! But visits do have to be handled with care to ensure that they don't look like victimisation to other employees. Conversely, reactions can be somewhat negative. Shocked by a particularly high level of absence one Monday, the personnel officer of Northern Ireland company European Components Corporation carried out a number of home visits: the resulting industrial action led to a softening of that particular approach (Arkin, 1992).

Return-to-work interviews

The second major policy aspect carried out by line managers is the return-to-work interview. According to the CBI (1997), nearly two thirds of the organisations in their most recent absence survey used return-to-work interviews as an integral part of their absence control strategies, and nearly three quarters of respondents reckoned that these interviews had a significant impact on absence levels. The CBI also analysed the overall absence levels in organisations which operated return-to-work interviews and compared them with those of organisations which did not. They found that absence levels were 20 per cent lower where return-to-work interviews operated.

Return-to-work interviews are normally conducted by the employee's immediate supervisor or manager and serve a number of purposes in absence control. First, they are concerned to identify the cause of the absence and may also provide an opportunity to explore any particular problems which the employee may have. Second, they serve to indicate to employees that their absence was noticed and that they were missed. A failure to carry out such an interview may indicate to staff that absences do not matter or that what is said in absence policies is not actually applied in practice. This, in turn, may serve to create a culture in which employees perceive that absence will be tolerated. The third purpose of a return-to-work interview, then, is to demonstrate that absence is a high priority for the employer and that stated policies are also put into practice.

It is important that return-to-work interviews are carried out by supervisors and managers after every instance of absence, without exception, and that they are carried out fairly and consistently. Supervisors and managers must be appropriately trained in how to conduct these interviews to help ensure that consistency is being achieved. Such training needs to focus on the techniques of 'problem-solving' interviews, and the use of counselling skills (see below) is likely to be appropriate. At Boots the Chemists (Industrial Society, 1997), for example, managers are required to

☐ enquire into the reason for the absence
☐ assess whether the reasons offered are consistent with other reliable available evidence
☐ raise any doubts with the member of staff
☐ allow the member of staff to explain the absence.

One of the difficulties experienced by organisations with policies of conducting return-to-work interviews is ensuring that they happen. Supervisors or managers find many competing pressures on their time and it may be tempting to overlook the requirement to carry out the interview. One approach is to install some control mechanism which requires documentary evidence or sign-off that the interview has taken place, such as a form to be returned to the personnel department. In any event it makes sense to keep some written record of the interview, which may become relevant if the formal disciplinary procedure needs to be invoked at a future date.

The carrot – rewards for good attendance

Rewards for good attendance take three forms: attendance bonuses, improved sick pay entitlements, and recognition. They all, in their different ways, aim to change employee attitudes to sickness.

Bonus schemes

Attendance bonuses offend the purist. Their reaction will be similar to the CBI's view (1989):

> The payment of attendance bonuses is contentious. Some employers have found the payment of bonuses to be a useful management tool. Other companies believe that attendance bonuses can engender a harmful set of attitudes, indicating that the company's requirement for attendance is not integral to the general requirements of employment and can penalise the genuinely sick. Other companies again have found attendance bonuses to have little beneficial effect after the 'novelty' value has worn off. It has also been argued that such schemes may encourage those who are unwell and who should not be at work to report for duty so as not to lose the bonus.

According to the CBI (1997) survey, bonus schemes operated in a third of their sample and were not thought particularly effective even by those who had them. In the authors' experience, however, employers with bonus schemes often think they do help reduce and hold down absence.

The real art seems to be in designing a bonus scheme which delivers a payment high enough to affect behaviour, but not too high that its withdrawal seriously affects income, especially for the genuinely sick.

Bonuses can be individual- or group-based, typically paying out every quarter or half year if absence is below a certain level or, in the case of individual bonuses, zero. IRS (1994) reported a number of options: a flat-rate cash bonus paid individually at British Coal; a weekly bonus for full attendance at Matthew County Chicken; a 'good attendance prize' for manual workers at Vaux Breweries equivalent to 25 per cent of a week's pay for no absence in a six-month period; and a bonus of up to £100 payable every six months at Borg-Warner based on £15 for each absence-free month, plus a further £10 if the employee has no absence at all in the six months.

There is a clear danger of paying for attendance twice, but since improved attendance does cut costs, is it fundamentally any different in reward terms from other improvements, such as reduced waste, greater accuracy in processing orders, or quicker delivery times? The Rover Group seemed to feel that there was no fundamental difference, according to an IDS study published in 1994. There, the scope for employees to earn two half-yearly bonuses recognised the contribution that lower absence made to reduced paybill costs. Payments arose from comparing actual absence levels with a target of zero absence. Starting at the then plant absence rate of 5 per cent, the scheme shared each 1 per cent improvement in absence equally between the company and employees: the employees were able to earn a maximum of $2^1/_2$ per cent extra pay for each six-month period. The bonus was earned only by those in full attendance over the period.

Such 'gainsharing' approaches are often based on continuous improvement. For example, if absence were reduced to 3 per cent, that becomes the base in the following year, and so on. Consequently, the scope for improvement gets tighter and tighter. Eventually, absence can cease to feature in the gain-sharing plan and bonuses switch to achieving other improvements (wastage, health and safety, customer care), although usually in these cases the new reduced level of absence must be maintained if the full bonus from the other source is to be earned. At that stage, pay linked to absence levels stops being a 'carrot' and becomes a 'stick'.

Occupational sick pay schemes

During the last few years more attention has been focused on the role that occupational sick pay schemes can play in helping to reduce absence. There have been three main reasons for this. First, there is the mundane. Some sick pay schemes actively encouraged absence (or at least, longer periods of absence). One company we know would not pay sick pay for single days of absence but would pay from the first day if absence was longer; the result – a high proportion of two-day absences. Another did not pay the first three days of sickness unless the absence exceeded two weeks; not surprisingly they found employees tending to take two weeks off to get the full payment.

Second, the introduction of statutory sick pay (SSP) and the subsequent withdrawal of the employers' rebate made employers more cost-conscious. Some chose to reduce the benefits from their own occupational scheme, tighten the eligibility rules, or introduce waiting days.

Third, for many reasons – multiskilling, delayering, devolution of responsibility, for instance – the trend recently has been to harmonise terms and conditions across the workforce. Treatment under company sick pay plans was often one of the major differences between blue- and white-collar workers. Bringing in one plan for both offered managers the opportunity to dangle in front of their manual employees the 'carrot' of more generous benefits for lower absence. Underpinned by a view that if manual employees wanted the same sick pay scheme as staff, they had to deliver the same (lower) rate of absence.

The Iveco Ford deal (Arkin, 1993) is a typical example of the *genre*. A high and rising manual absence rate problem was coupled with the need to introduce a new sick pay scheme. Part of the deal agreed with the unions offered the prospect of full payment for the first three days of sickness provided that the plant absence level fell below 3.5 per cent (the white-collar rate) in the previous six months. Although based on a plant-wide target, access to payment from day one is not available to employees if they have been absent on two or more occasions for a total of 20 days over the previous 12 months.

The effect has been beneficial, as the case-study at the end of this book shows. But the arrangement did highlight a problem: every time absence fell below 3.5 per cent, and employees became eligible for sick pay from day one, the absence rate would rise again. So the rate would yo-yo between 3.5 per cent and 5 per cent as access to the sick pay scheme was achieved and lost again. (One answer to this problem might have been to move to an individual rather than a group target.) Borg-Warner Automotive operated a system by which the frequency and length of absence in a year determined the standard of sick pay scheme the employee would be entitled to in the following year (IRS, 1994). Such an approach has advantages but might weaken the peer group pressures that keep employees in line.

Another option might be to reduce the 'swing' between three and no waiting days by linking particular absence triggers to different numbers of waiting days – for example, absence at 5 per cent to three waiting days, 4 per cent to two waiting days, 3 per cent to one waiting day, and to no waiting days if absence over a given period is below 3 per cent. This would undoubtedly be complex to operate, but such an approach would smooth out the linkage between absence rates and waiting days.

Recognition

Other forms of rewarding low absence rates other than cash can also be beneficial. Non-pecuniary rewards include sending letters of appreciation to employees with no absence during a given period, or non-cash prizes such as a dinner or vouchers for goods. Often, non-pecuniary approaches operate alongside other absence policies to reinforce the message that absence does matter to the organisation.

...Or the stick: formal and informal sanctions for poor attenders

Employers can use a range of formal and informal sanctions against poor attenders. The more draconian of these – disciplinary procedures and dismissal – are the subject of the next chapter. Other approaches are merely the reverse of the 'carrots'. For example, access to better sick pay entitlements acts as a spur to better attendance, while the threat of reduced entitlements helps to maintain improvements. Similarly, losing attendance bonuses penalises absence in the opposite way that paying bonuses rewards attendance.

Two other approaches have also been adopted by employers. One concerns the recruitment process – namely, the avoidance of recruiting potential poor attenders in the first place, and the need to induct new employees in a low absence culture; the other concerns using attendance as a criterion for selection for redundancy.

Recruitment, selection and induction

It was noted in Chapter 2 that past absence behaviour – particularly the frequency of absence spells – is a fairly reliable indicator of future absences, and it is therefore sensible to consider what can be done to screen out poor attenders during the recruitment and selection process. According to the CBI's (1997) survey, around two thirds of organisations take steps to avoid the recruitment of poor attendees and 60 per cent of respondents thought that this was effective in reducing absence. The Industrial Society's (1994) study of organisational practices advises that the following measures should be considered:

- □ asking for information about absence on the application form
- □ asking about the number of days lost through absence over the last year or two at the interview (but avoiding or discounting revelations of pregnancy or disability-related absence which may breach discrimination legislation)
- □ asking specifically about attendance levels in a reference request
- □ using 'job previews' to help ensure that all applicants fully understand the job, its pressures and its working environment before they accept
- □ using pre-employment medical screening to focus on any health problems
- □ ensuring that the importance of regular attendance and absence notification procedures are fully explained at induction
- □ closely monitoring attendance levels during a new employee's probationary period.

One organisation which uses pre-employment health questionnaires is Bass Brewers (Arkin, 1997). The screening of the completed questionnaires is carried out on the company's behalf by a specialist health consultancy who advises the company on whether an applicant should have a full examination on the basis of the information provided. In the company's opinion, health screening plays a part in keeping absence levels down and, with absence rates of 2.5 per cent amongst white-collar staff and 3.5 per cent amongst manual employees, the company's record compares favourably with the UK average.

A word of caution needs to be sounded, however, about the implications of pre-employment health screening in the light of the Disability Discrimination Act (1995), which came into force in December 1996. According to employment lawyer Gillian Howard, employers need to take care in using pre-employment screening information to reject applicants without enquiring into the reasons underlying any absences reported. If absences relate to disability and an applicant is rejected without further enquiries, this could amount to discrimination under the Disability Discrimination Act. She advises that employers should not use pre-employment screening to reject applicants, but rather that applicants should be professionally screened by occupational health physicians who know the exact requirements of the post.

Absence as a criterion for redundancy selection

The CBI (1997) found that nearly half of all organisations replying to their absence survey used absence as a criterion for redundancy selection. This confirms the recent trend away from the traditional 'last in, first out' approach to redundancy and towards the use of multiple criteria for redundancy selection, sometimes based on weighting and scores attached to each criterion (Fowler, 1993; IRS, 1995b). While it would be unusual to use absence as the sole criterion for redundancy selection, IRS (1995b) identified the criteria used by a majority of employers as a combination of skills, performance and attendance. The use of attendance records has the advantage that the information is potentially objective and attendance criteria can be applied consistently. Fowler (1993) cautions that attendance records must be reliable, or there could be a risk of unfair selection, and mitigating circumstances – for example, personal circumstances causing temporary absence problems for employees with previously good records – must be taken into account. Care needs to be taken to use absence data which, on the one hand, go back a sufficient time period to avoid this situation, but on the other do not go back so far that historical absence problems are taken into account for redundancy selection even though the problem has long been rectified. Moreover, if any currently long-term sick employees are to be made redundant, industrial tribunals expect that the proper procedures, reviewed in Chapter 4, have been followed. Overall, Fowler advises that attendance should be only one factor in redundancy selection, but recent evidence of organisational practice suggests that it is a factor which is increasingly used.

Flexible working arrangements and job redesign

It was noted in Chapter 2 that absence is affected not just by employees' motivation to attend but by their ability to attend because of family, domestic or travel problems. Now that increasing numbers of employees are combining work and family roles (such as caring for children or elderly relatives), there is some logic in introducing flexibility in working hours or patterns in order to accommodate them. A wide variety of flexible working patterns have emerged in the last 10 to 20 years, and a number of these have relevance for absence control.

Part-time working and jobsharing

Part-time working has been growing significantly in recent years, up from 15 per cent of the total workforce in the early 1970s to 25 per cent today; more than eight of every ten part-timers are female. Jobsharing is a variation on traditional part-time working which enables a full-time job to be split so that it can be performed by two or more jobholders in a way that the total weekly hours required can be covered by some agreed pattern, such as split days (one jobholder working mornings and the other afternoons), split weeks (one jobholder covering the first part of the week and the other the second) or alternate weeks (Evans and Attew, 1986). According to the Industrial Society (1997), a third of organisations offer jobsharing arrangements, although a survey by IRS (*Employment Trends*, June 1997) puts the figure higher, at 50 per cent. One significant advantage of part-time working and jobsharing is that they more readily enable time to be allocated to work and non-work roles, and consequently less time is taken off during working hours. Absence surveys unfortunately do not provide a very clear picture as to whether this is so because they do not provide a breakdown of full- and part-time employees for comparable occupational groups. The balance of the evidence available, however, indicates that part-timers have slightly lower absence rates than full-timers. The Industrial Society (1997), for example, found that part-timers had a median absence rate of 2.86 per cent compared with 2.94 per cent for full-timers, and the CBI (1997) found absence rates lower amongst part-time than full-time manual workers, but slightly higher rates for part-time non-manuals compared with their full-time equivalents.

Flexitime

In existence in Britain since the 1960s, flexitime schemes were found by the Industrial Society (1997) survey of absence and attendance practices to operate in just over a third of organisations. Such schemes usually provide for a fixed number of core hours around which employees have flexibility to vary start and finish times and the length of lunch breaks. They often incorporate facilities for employees to work longer hours if they wish and build up an additional leave allowance which can be used to meet emergencies. Flexitime therefore provides scope for employees to adapt working hours to meet their personal requirements and accumulate a buffer of time off for unexpected contingencies.

All the evidence indicates that flexitime schemes have proved highly effective in reducing absence levels. For example, Dalton and Mesch (1990) found that absence rates fell by about a quarter in the year following the introduction of flexitime amongst one group of employees in an American public utility company, while they remained constant amongst employees not receiving the benefit. Moreover, when the scheme was subsequently withdrawn after running for a year, absence levels returned to their former levels. Rhodes and Steers (1990) report a range of studies of the impact of flexitime on absence, almost all of which resulted in lower levels.

Another variant on flexible working hours is the four-and-a- half-day week, with a lunchtime finish on Friday, which became quite widespread in UK manufacturing industry during the 1980s. Huczynski and Fitzpatrick (1989) report that at one company adopting this approach, Warner Lambert, absence fell by about a quarter, and at another, Baxi Heating, 'significant improvements' were achieved on previous absence levels.

Temporal flexibility

Since the mid-1980s, in addition to the long-established flex-itime schemes, a wide range of flexible working patterns have emerged which are sometimes referred to under the banner of 'temporal flexibility'. In essence, these involve a shift away from the tradition that employment contracts require employees to work a standard number of hours per day and standard number of days per week and towards much greater flexibility of hours which change according to the demands of the business. Depending on exactly how business demands vary, a number of organisations have introduced flexible working hours arrangements whereby hours of work vary by the day, the week or the month according to a predefined pattern, while others have established flexible annual hours arrangements which enable employers to vary hours of work according to demand during the course of a year.

The Industrial Society (1997) found that 36 per cent of organisations operated flexible working hours, 13 per cent of them worked annual hours and 10 per cent used term-time working. The key findings were that employers felt that these approaches did help reduce absence, and that this was confirmed when checking the absence rates of organisations with these policies against the average. A by-product of annual hours arrangements in particular, and one often mentioned by employers, is its effect in reducing absence. IDS in their study of annual hours arrangements in 1996 commented:

> Employers who have implemented annual hours have found the main advantages to be the ability to meet fluctuating production requirements, increased productivity, more flexibility to adapt working time to overcome problems such as absenteeism, improved cost control of salaries and removal of the 'overtime culture'.

Employers attribute the effect on absence levels to peer group pressure, for staff on standby at home have to come to work to cover for absent colleagues, so that some of the 'cost' of absence, in the sense of lost leisure-time, is borne by employees rather than the employer.

Flexible annual leave arrangements

There has been a trend in recent years to move away from granting additional leave for 'special' purposes, such as medical appointments, family sickness or other short-term domestic problems at a manager's discretion towards formalising any such entitlement as part of written policy. So, for example, as basic holiday entitlement has increased, more employers have adopted a policy of requiring special leave needs to be met from basic entitlement or from some separate leave entitlement set aside for this purpose (Long and Hill, 1988). The Industrial Society (1997) found that nearly one third of employers surveyed had flexible annual leave arrangements and that over 60 per cent of respondents felt that such a policy was effective in reducing absence levels.

Working from home

There has been a growth in interest in recent years in the topics of homeworking and 'teleworking' (working from home via a computer terminal linked to the employer's 'host' computer), although it is unclear how many people actually work under such an arrangement. The opportunity to work from home provides the maximum flexibility to organise working time so as to combine work and non-work roles. In principle, it goes a long way towards removing the problems associated with the 'ability to attend' such as travel difficulties, adverse weather problems, the illness of family members or an array of other domestic constraints. Although we know of no study of absence levels amongst home or teleworkers, it seems highly likely that this mode of working would be an effective means of reducing absence. A related development reported by the Industrial Society (1997) is an apparent increase in employers' flexibility to permit employees to work from home occasionally, a policy adopted by a quarter of employers surveyed. Over half of the managers who responded to the survey felt that such a policy was also effective in contributing to lower absence levels.

Job design and teamworking

The prevailing approach to job design has been broadly based upon the ideas of 'scientific management', but over the past two or three decades alternative models of work design have been offered. Job enrichment, proposed by Herzberg (1966) focused mainly on the redesign of individual jobs and incorporated many of the elements of what today has become generally known as 'empowerment'. Enriched jobs consist of a complete set of related tasks rather than fragmented ones. Greater responsibility and authority for decision-making are delegated to the jobholder with less close supervision, and opportunities are created for jobholders to learn new skills and perform new tasks. Hackman and Oldham (1975) in a similar vein propose that jobs should contain the 'core dimensions' of skill variety, autonomy and responsibility for outcomes and feedback on results. Similar proposals were put by the Tavistock Institute (Trist, 1963), but their focus was more on 'autonomous' work groups rather than individuals. An autonomous work group should thus experience minimal supervision with devolved responsibility for work standards, be responsible for a complete cycle of activities that result in some meaningful end product (or service) and have opportunities to acquire and use a range of skills and knowledge. More recently, there has been a considerable growth in interest in ideas of teamworking, also known as 'high-performance' or 'self-managing' work teams which, according to the CBI (1997), now operate in two thirds of organisations surveyed. These emerged during the 1980s as a central part of organisations' strategies for adapting and surviving in a highly competitive environment, especially, but not exclusively, in manufacturing. Some of the key characteristics of high-performance work groups include (Buchanan in Salaman, 1992, p.148):

☐ multiskilled, flexible work roles
☐ flexible work systems so that skills can be redeployed as required

- [ ] delayered management structures
- [ ] rigorous approaches to recruitment and selection, including the use of psychometric tests and sometimes assessment centres for all employees
- [ ] encouraging and rewarding the acquisition and deployment of new skills and knowledge, often supported by modular training systems and skills or competence-based pay
- [ ] a high degree of self-management, minimal supervision and broader spans of control amongst supervisory and management staff
- [ ] greater devolvement of responsibility for work methods, work arrangements and quality of output to team level, with a focus on the use of group problem-solving techniques (eg quality circles)
- [ ] changes in the role of managers from one of close supervision to a more open style, and a greater emphasis on the role of manager as coach, facilitator, mentor and source of advice and support for the team.

While job enrichment, empowerment and teamworking have a range of potential benefits for organisations, what conclusions can be reached about their impact on absence? In a review of research into the impact of job enrichment generally, Rhodes and Steers (1990) note that nine out of 13 experiments reviewed produced decreases in absence, with a median decrease of 14.5 per cent following the implementation of job enrichment. In studies of job redesign involving autonomous work groups, they found that of the 24 studies that mentioned the level of absence as an outcome, 81 per cent reported reductions in absence. Where the initiatives involved the development of employees' technical skills, 100 per cent of studies mentioned absence reduction as an outcome.

They note in conclusion that, of the approaches to job redesign, autonomous work groups are more likely than job enrichment to impact on absence behaviour. This is because autonomous work groups tend to be associated with significant changes in the culture, structure and processes of the organisation. They are characterised by high trust, involve workers in the change process, bring about highly interdependent work roles, and establish clear group objectives and standards. Since absence, particularly in frequent short spells, is likely to disrupt the cohesion of the group in achieving its objectives, they are more likely to develop cultures in which peer pressures are brought to bear on absentees.

The potential role of work groups in enforcing discipline through peer pressure has also been raised by Edwards and Whiston (1989) who observed:

> The rise of 'participation' and 'flexibility' ... is often seen as implying a disciplinary system in which self-reliance replaces the enforcement of rules. A reasonable further inference is that active policing is no longer needed.

A number of examples of the role of work group discipline in the workplace can be quoted. Peter Wickens, in his book *The Road To Nissan* (1987), notes that the company (in the context of timekeeping) 'has replaced the bureaucratic approach of time clocks with an atmosphere of trust and self-generated discipline within the work group'. If a group becomes responsible for maintaining good standards of punctuality through peer pressure, why not also good standards of attendance? Whether connected with group pressure or not, Nissan is reported in the press as experiencing absence levels of 3 per cent compared with a UK motor industry norm of 10 per cent.

Similar findings are offered by Drago and Wooden (1992). They note that there are two possible outcomes from the existence of strong cohesive work group norms. Workers either feel greater loyalty towards each other than to the firm and engage in anti-firm behaviour – for example, by establishing high absence norms. Or they feel greater loyalty to the firm and engage in co-operative behaviour, generating high commitment and enforcing low absence norms. The key variables are group cohesion and job satisfaction. Group cohesion relates to the extent to which group members feel part of a team and get on well together where the job requires mutual co-operation. Drago and Wooden (*ibid*, p.776) conclude:

> Workgroup norms largely control whether absence events occur ... with workgroup cohesion leading to low absence where job satisfaction is high and high absence where job satisfaction is low.

Other examples may also be cited. Iveco Ford Trucks halved its absence rate by using peer pressure to stop unwarranted absence (Arkin, 1993). Boots the Chemists believe that operating small teams of four to five people helps to keep absence low (Industrial Society, 1994). There is a similar belief in the value of small teams in controlling absence at IBC Vehicles. Here, each team consists of six people, with a team leader. Team members are mutually reliant and cover for each other's absence. There is also an award for the team that scores the highest number of points, which are scored for attendance levels as well as for housekeeping and quality. More recently, the CBI's survey of absence found a sharp rise in teamworking from 34 per cent of organisations in 1994 to 65 per cent in 1996. As regards the impact of teamworking on absence, 70 per cent of managers believed that it had been effective in reducing it. We may conclude, therefore, that work group norms, cultures and the increasing use of self-managing teams with mutually interdependent roles appear to make a significant impact on absence levels.

Helping employees with family commitments

The CBI (1997) notes that employers rated family responsibilities the second highest factor overall contributing to absence. It was a medium to high factor for 45 per cent of manual workers and 49 per cent of non-manuals. Many of the flexible working arrangements outlined in the preceding section recognise one objective to be to work with the grain of employees' family commitments. Term-time working, working at home, flexitime, or working hours to fit in with the school day all allow parents better scope to balance their work and their families. Another option is based on providing help with child care whether on- or off-site. But these cannot address the problem of caring for sick relatives and the one-off occasional need to take children to the dentist, for example. Some companies recognise these demands by having some a form of contingency measures to meet these eventualities. Such an approach does not reduce absence as such, but it creates an atmosphere where the employee is not obliged to lie about why he or she was absent. It also helps establish the image of a caring employer.

Both effects help improve morale and create an environment where unnecessary absence can be properly identified and dealt with.

Occupational health programmes and absence counselling

All of our case-studies back up their absence policies with efforts to promote healthy lifestyles. The CBI (1997) found around half of employers offered occupation health services and/or health promotion or education. On the CBI's calculation both approaches were more or less neutral in their impact on absence. The earlier Industrial Society survey (1993) broke provision down into more specific approaches. It found that three quarters of organisations had health screening for some or all employees; 69 per cent offered 'healthy meals' in their canteens; and 39 per cent provided sports facilities.

There has been a tendency in the past to consider occupational health generally as a blue-collar issue. That is, provision of occupational health measures was seen largely as addressing physiological problems arising from manual work. For example, the major cause of absence at Royal Mail was musculo-skeletal problems which were tackled by paying for injured staff to visit a physiotherapist. This is undoubtedly an important problem: it is estimated that 106 million days are lost each year to back pain.

However, 90 million days are lost through stress. There is growing evidence that mental health problems contribute to absence levels, particularly among white-collar workers. In fact, a broad breakdown of employers' assessments of the causes of absence suggests that marginally more (54 per cent) are put down to mental issues. A major factor seems to be increased stress. Employers in the CBI (1997) survey reckoned that work-related stress was a significant cause of absence for 22 per cent of manual workers and 35 per cent of white-collar employees. Though they note that this is somewhat down on the 1995 survey results, the figures refer only to work-related stress. Stress leading to absence may come from other causes such as family commitments, divorce, and even moving house.

Speaking at a recent conference, Dr David Costain, Deputy

Medical Director of BUPA, said that most company spending on health focuses on the effects of ill-health, not the causes – that is, most of it is tactical rather than strategic. He suggested a three-pronged approach to health management based on measuring the current health and wellbeing of the workforce; reviewing data and identifying key health issues and related costs; and targeting specific health-care interventions.

Promoting healthy lifestyles (including smoking and drug abuse policies), retaining occupational health advice accessible to employees, using pre- and post-employment medicals, encouraging a proper attitude to health and safety at work, ergonomically redesigning jobs to reduce physical strains, and ensuring that employees at least have a choice of healthy food in the canteen, are all on-going strategies employers could use to keep their workforces physically fitter. Keeping them mentally fitter may be more difficult. Job enrichment and empowerment policies help to reduce tedium and raise self-regard, and training employees in stress and time management may help them at least contain the problem. Employers could also look to flexible working arrangements to help employees balance the competing demands upon them. But probably the biggest change needs to come from employers themselves, a change to corporate cultures which recognise the increasing demands being placed on employees and which seek to do something about it.

Absence counselling

Absence counselling is an important way of helping employees to identify the causes of absence, any related problems, and how these may be overcome. Counselling interviews are often triggered when certain specified absence criteria have been exceeded. In order to ensure that the criteria are monitored and counselling interviews are carried out consistently, computerised personnel systems are often used to track cumulative absences in a given period and generate 'diary' reminders to personnel staff that action is due. Systems may also have facilities to generate the relevant letter to the supervisor or manager to remind him or her to arrange a counselling interview.

It is important to be clear how a counselling interview differs from a return-to-work interview and from the first stage of the formal disciplinary procedure. The main focus of a return-to-work interview is on the cause of the particular absence in question and, where appropriate, its connections with a pattern of absences which may have been observed, with an emphasis on solving the immediate problem. A counselling interview is likely to be more broad-ranging and take considerably more time than the return-to-work interview, although in practice the difference between the two may not always be clear-cut. Procedurally, counselling often follows a series of return-to-work interviews which have not proved effective in altering the absence behaviour, but clearly precedes the first stage of the disciplinary procedure, which is likely to be invoked if the counselling interview is similarly ineffective. Counselling is not about applying formal disciplinary sanctions, and it is important if it is to be effective that it is not perceived as such. It is about setting aside sufficient time and applying relevant counselling skills. It should also be clearly distinguished from professional counselling, unless the interview is conducted by trained counsellors under the auspices of an 'employee assistance programme'.

The essence of counselling in a workplace is to encourage employees to recognise that there is a problem and to help them come up with a solution which meets the needs of both employer and employee. Following an initial statement of the problem, the emphasis should be on encouraging employees to present their perceptions of the issue and to come up with courses of action that they are prepared to commit to. Effective counselling interviews should not be restricted to a discussion of the immediate issues in hand, but encourage a wide focus so that other related or underlying problems can be identified. For example, the cause of frequent short absences may be the result of family, financial or other non-work-related pressures or because of problems in the workplace not otherwise apparent. Depending on the resources available to the employer, the result of counselling may be the provision of some further assistance with dealing with a problem. In any event, counselling should result in an agreed action plan to which the supervisor and the employee is committed, which states what further support will be provided (eg training), sets targets for achievement, and makes provision for monitoring and review. The employee should be left in no doubt that any further failure to improve will result in formal disciplinary action, and this, together with the agreed actions, should be confirmed in writing.

Involving employees and trade unions

Case-study evidence suggests that employers have actively tried to involve their employees and trade unions in designing and enforcing absence policies. IRS (1994) found that over a third of organisations provided absence statistics to their trade unions. The starting-point for attacking absence at Iveco was a sharing of information about absence with trade unions leading to a new absence policy based around access to the sick pay scheme, both agreed with the unions.

Employers say that unions often support management's attempts to control absence not least, as Iveco found, because they tend to get all the flak from members' having to cover for absent colleagues. Usually the unions' primary objective is to ensure that policies are fair and equitable, not to condone unreasonable absence. The introduction of a computerised personnel system at European Components Corporation provided the ammunition which eventually forced the unions to acknowledge the scale of the absence problem at the company and to support management in its efforts to tackle the problem.

Some organisations have found that involving individual employees is also valuable. Attitude surveys can pinpoint the existence of an absence problem, help assess employees' own attitudes to absence, and identify approaches that might reduce it. There are plenty of anecdotal stories to suggest that employees dislike malingerers as much as employers: when managers choose to discipline those running taxi firms while on sick leave, or attending Test Matches in full view of the cameras, they are more likely to get employee support than not. But it is *management's* job to tackle absence, and it is unreasonable to expect employees to do it for them – if managers turn a blind eye to absence, so will employees. What managers can get through involving employees is their support for actions they see as fair and reasonable – and for policies to work, that seems essential.

Having said that, employers with 'carrot'-type incentives to reduce absence – especially where the benefit is earned in relation to group performance – find that employee peer group pressure can be an important tool. Where all employees stand to lose a bonus, access to a generous sick pay scheme, or free time, they do appear to exert a pressure on individuals to keep sick absence to a minimum. While this is a healthy attitude to foster, employers need to be on their guard that peer group pressure is not resulting in discrimination against groups perceived to be likely to have high absence rates (the chronically sick, or some people with disabilities), nor that it forces the genuinely ill to come in to work.

Trigger points

Absence policies often consist of a number of stages starting with informal interviews and running through a gamut of formal warnings and referrals to occupational health practitioners to the ultimate sanction of dismissal. Guidance for managers usually sets out the sort of absence record which triggers each stage (although, of course, the disciplinary procedure can come in at any stage if there is real abuse). This is not always the case, though, and some organisations apply the absence policy on a case-by-case basis or take account of where an individual's absence differs from the normal pattern of absence.

The use of triggers is widespread. About three quarters of the organisations in the IRS (1994) survey used them. They fall into four groupings. These need not be mutually exclusive, however, as different sorts of absence may have different triggers for different policy prescriptions. Although the triggers are collectively applied in that they are typically company-, department- or group-wide, it is individuals who usually trip the trigger and to whom the absence policy is applied. This is not always the case. At Iveco Ford breach of the absence trigger giving access to the company sick pay schemes affects the sick pay entitlement of all the relevant employees; even if the trigger is not breached individual employees may have their entitlement removed if they have been absent sick on two or more occasions amounting to 20 days' absence in the last 12 months.

The most obvious trigger is one based on *the length of sick leave*, where an absence of over 10 working days might lead to a general review of the individual's record by the line manager and/or personnel department and to a referral to an occupational health service. At Alliance and Leicester Building Society, 10 days' absence over a four-week period leads to a review, whereas Fisons' employees absent for 10 days or longer are referred to the occupational health department (IRS, 1994). A slight variation on this theme is the use of a percentage absence target to determine access to the company sick pay scheme as at Iveco Ford.

Perhaps more common are triggers based on *the number of spells of absence*. A review might be automatically triggered when an employee is absent x number of times in y months. Practice varies. At Courtaulds European Fibres a computer report is generated after four instances of absence in a 12-month period; five separate instances in the past 12 months at Norwich and Peterborough Building Society; or three absences in a three-month period at Northumberland County Council. These approaches fit more closely with measures of absence based on the Bradford Factor (see Chapter 1), where reviews are undertaken once an individual's Bradford points score exceeds certain thresholds. At Vosper Thorneycroft, for example, if an individual's points score exceeds 130 his or her absence may be investigated (IRS, 1994). An early approach used at Rover Group related various stages to the Bradford score over a 52-week period as follows (IDS: 1994b):

Points	Action
200 or above	Recorded formal warning
1,250 or above	Attendance improvement letter*
3,500 or above	Final attendance improvement letter*
7,500+	Dismissal review
	* with at least two spells of absence

Some organisations use *a combination* of frequency and spells as their triggers – for example, seven days *or* three absences in a 12-month period. The procedure at Co-operative Bank is to review after 15 days' continuous absence or three spells in a three-month period; Powergen Drakelow use seven days or three absences over the latest 12 months; and Doncaster Metropolitan Borough Council uses 15 days or five separate occasions (IRS, 1994). Royal Mail Scotland and Northern Ireland have a three-staged approach leading up to and including dismissal:

Stage	Trigger
1	4 absences or 14 days' sick leave in a 12-month period
2	2 absences or 10 days' sick leave in the next six months
3	2 absences or 10 days lost in any six-month period in the 12 months after a stage 2 warning.

Finally, some organisations look for a *pattern* – ie regularly taking off certain days of the week or year. (Such patterns can point to other genuine health problems such as alcohol abuse.) Yorkshire Bank investigates short absences totalling 10 to 15 days, especially where absence precedes or follows weekends.

Whatever triggers are used, they have to be acted on. Royal Mail monitor their absence procedure by analysing whether line managers do actually take action once the triggers are activated.

Which policies work best?

The $64,000 question at the end of all this is about about which absence control policies work best – that is, which are most effective in reducing absence without, equally crucially, affecting the performance of the business. An example: a policy that bullied a genuinely ill person into attending work, thus spreading 'flu around the office, could hardly be considered a roaring success. Similarly, policies that seem unfair to employees by penalising the genuinely sick may be bad for morale and for work attitudes. The defining line between successful and unsuccessful policies can be very fine. But the policies outlined in this chapter and implemented in a range of companies, including the case-studies at the end of this book, do lower absence rates.

There are many examples of policies that have helped to bring down absence levels. At Iveco Ford the rate has halved from 7 per cent to $3\frac{1}{2}$ per cent. Even more spectacular was the reduction at Lewisham Council, where the rate fell from around 16 per cent to nearer 4 per cent. Fiddlers Ferry Power Station saw their absence rate fall from 13 per cent to 2.2 per cent (CBI/HAY, 1994).

Self-evidently, absence policies do reduce absence. But employers do favour some policies over others. Which are they, and which do they think are most effective?

Absence policies – the employers' view

The recent CBI (1997) absence survey found that the most popular absence policies (including policies that may indirectly affect absence) were formal notification procedures (90 per cent of employers operated such a system), disciplinary procedures (85 per cent), provision of absence statistics to line managers (65 per cent), teamworking (65 per cent), steps to avoid the recruitment of potential poor attenders (64 per cent), return-to-work interviews (63 per cent), and pre-recruitment medicals (62 per cent).

Employers also tend to give these policies very high scores in terms of their ability to reduce absence. Table 1 shows the percentage of employers who give policies a medium to high rating as absence reducers.

By and large, employers' beliefs about the effectiveness of different policies and practices is directly related to their use. For example, the attendance bonus scored lowest for effectiveness and was the least used absence policy amongst the CBI survey sample. However, it is worth noticing that return-to-work interviews came only sixth in incidence of usage (this policy was used by 63 per cent of employers) despite its achieving the highest effectiveness score.

In 1993, when the authors of this book worked on the first CBI/Percom absence survey, they carried out a cross-correlation in the confident knowledge that companies with the most comprehensive package of policies would enjoy the lowest absence rates. They therefore assessed the absence rates

Table 1

EMPLOYERS' RATING OF THE EFFECTIVENESS OF ABSENCE POLICIES

Policy	% Giving medium to high score for effectiveness
Formal notification procedures	82
Disciplinary procedures	69
Provision of absence statistics to line managers	69
Teamworking	70
Avoiding recruitment of poor attenders	60
Return-to-work interviews	73
Pre-recruitment medicals	56
Occupational health services	58
Health promotion	43
Absence as a criterion for selection for redundancy	28
Waiting days before OSP is paid	35
Attendance bonuses	34

Source: *Managing Absence*, CBI/BUPA/MCG, 1997

in organisations which had each individual policy with the absence rates of those that did not. The results were disappointing. For every policy, except one, we found a negative relationship. That is, organisations with particular policies had *higher* absence rates than those without. The only exception was using the previous absence record as a determinant for redundancy. This phenomenon was confirmed in both the subsequent CBI/Percom surveys (1994 and 1995).

It is again confirmed in the latest CBI survey, but with two important differences. Now, although using individual absence records in choosing people for redundancy still has the best relationship to lower absence rates, more policies have a positive correlation. Table 2 sets out the average difference in absence rates between organisations in which a particular policy did or did not operate; the figures show the percentage amount by which the absence rate was lower (+) or higher (–) where a particular policy existed compared to organisations without such a policy.

Table 2

PERCENTAGE DIFFERENCE IN ABSENCE RATES IN RELATION TO POLICY OPERATING

Policy	% Difference
Absence as a criterion for selection for redundancy	+20
Disciplinary procedures	+13
Teamworking	+11
Health promotion	+6
Pre-recruitment medicals	+2
Avoiding recruitment of poor attenders	+1
Formal notification procedures	−
Occupational health services	−8
Waiting days before OSP is paid	−15
Provision of absence statistics to managers line	−17
Return-to-work interviews	−20
Attendance bonuses	−24

Source: *Managing Absence*, CBI/BUPA/MCG, 1997

Some interesting results emerge. Formal notification procedures – the most common absence control policy and the one rated most effective by employers – comes seventh in terms of its impact on absence according to the CBI's calculations; whereas using absence as a determinant for redundancy was rated only tenth by employers but actually scores highest in the CBI analysis. Health promotion is also much more effective than employers think. On the other hand, employers think attendance bonuses are pretty ineffective, and it seems they are right.

But the figures must be treated with caution. First, we can expect smaller employers to have the least sophisticated absence management policies, but this is the group which, for reasons outlined elsewhere, already has the lowest absence records so it tends to bias the results. Second, the survey represents the state of play at a point in time: we know nothing about the level of absence before the policy was introduced, so the absence rates may be higher in companies with particular policies but lower than they might otherwise have been. Third, the CBI analysis is based on a national sample. Possibly within particular industries organisations with policies do enjoy a lower absence than their competitors who do not have the policies. Finally, almost by definition, organisations which have used voluntary redundancy programmes to weed out employees with high absence are likely to have below average absence rates. This point was observed in relation to Iveco Ford Trucks where the personnel manager acknowledged that the absence rate might have fallen as a result of a voluntary redundancy programme which saw many of those with poor attendance records being invited to 'volunteer' to leave (Arkin, 1993).

The evidence may appear to undermine accepted wisdom, but we must not lose sight of the fact that individual companies have found that adopting the right policies does reduce absence. The art is finding the right mix for you.

Absence policies – the employees' view

Very little research has been done into employees' attitudes to absence policies and the approaches they think most likely to succeed. More recently employers have started to take account of employee expectations in designing policies. Royal Mail Scotland and Northern Ireland used an opinion survey of employees to find out what really made the difference in creating an 'attendance' culture and have acted on the results (see case-study). Other organisations have also gone down the attitude survey route, not only to get employee views on policies but, more importantly, to assess the degree to which employees themselves 'disapprove' of absence levels. Trade unions represent another important conduit of employee discontent; often union officials are only too well aware of absence problems because their members have to cover for absent colleagues and are generally not too happy about it. Employers note that unions rarely have a problem with management's wish to tackle absence, but do want to ensure that policies are fair to their members who are genuinely ill. Many employers, including those in our case-studies, have determined absence policies with their employee representatives.

Generally, however, employers often have only a subliminal view about staff attitudes to absence. Most note that staff know who the malingerers are and want the problem dealt with. But few, we suspect, have ever bothered to find out how their employees want to see the issue handled.

Research into employee attitudes to sickness policies carried out by Harvey and Nicholson in 1993 gives some useful pointers. The research was based on a survey of about 1,300 officers in one region of a civil service department. It was built around two fundamental questions asking whether individuals felt there should be (a) an incentive, or (b) a penalty to encourage/discourage poor attendance. If the answer to either question was 'yes' the respondent was asked to indicate the shape of the incentive or penalty. Individuals were also asked to comment generally on the policies on offer. It is worth noting that as far as penalties were concerned, they thought these should not apply to those generally ill; and several opposed incentives on the grounds that attendance was part of what they were paid for already. Moving to the specific, the perceived effectiveness of the two approaches clearly varied with seniority: lower-grade staff tended to favour incentives (although penalties also figured large), but the emphasis given to penalties (and lack of emphasis given to incentives) rose consistently as one moved up the grading structure. In terms of each approach, the preferred incentive was a cash award, and the preferred penalty a warning. The authors note that this might imply that the employees individually saw themselves as more likely to earn the award than get a penalty!

Similarly, the preferences also varied with age, although of course this also links into grade, in that older people were less likely to favour incentives than young people, and *vice versa* when it came to penalties. This might reflect the fact that other evidence on attendance patterns shows young people prone to take a comparatively high number of short absences, whereas older people are more likely to have one-off breaks for long-term illness. Perhaps younger employees acknowledge that their absences are less legitimate and therefore could be 'bought out', whereas older people are more likely to be genuinely ill, and therefore feel that incentives would be inappropriate. Similarly, older people *know* their young colleagues are swinging the lead and feel they should be penalised, while it would be unfair to treat their genuine illness in the same way.

The authors drew a number of important conclusions about the employees' perceptions of absence policies:

☐ Although employees give a more than expected emphasis to penalties, they nevertheless do not believe the genuinely ill should be penalised.
☐ Employees would appreciate recognition of good attendance – although it is not clear whether this has to be tangible or intangible.
☐ Employees have a powerful sense of what is fair.
☐ Measures will work best if they have some 'utility' for the employee; if they are perceived as negative or unfair, employees may react against them.

Conclusion

Employers have a raft of absence policies at their disposal, and each one – to some degree and dependent on circumstances – can help reduce absence levels. Guidelines for implementing policies are covered in Chapter 5. Four important points from this review of policies are worth emphasising here. First, creating an attendance culture is as important, if not more important, than just setting out to control absence. Second, line managers are crucial to success but they can't just be left to get on with it; they must be given training, guidance and support at all stages. Third, policies seem to work better if they take account of employee attitudes and needs. Finally, absence can reflect something else – lax management, boring work, family difficulties – alongside just illness; find out what *really* causes absence in your organisation and you are long way towards solving it.

4

THE DISCIPLINARY AND LEGAL FRAMEWORK OF ABSENCE MANAGEMENT

The obligations of employees to attend and the rights of employers to invoke disciplinary sanctions stem from the contract of employment, and the opening part of this chapter therefore takes this as an essential starting-point for considering how absence is to be managed. In particular, employers need to consider what their contractual provisions are in relation to attendance standards, and also audit their procedures to ensure that they are fair and comply with the statutory provisions. As part of their review of contractual provisions on standards of attendance some employers have introduced measurable standards, as discussed under 'Trigger points' in Chapter 3.

When dealing with absence at the workplace, three important matters need to be considered, and these will form the bulk of the remainder of the chapter. The first issue relates to whether a contract has been frustrated as the result of a long-term sickness absence. The second concerns the procedures to be followed when attempting to deal with the issue of long-term sickness generally. Finally, the third concerns the procedures for handling frequent short-term absences.

The contract of employment

The contract of employment sets out the rights, duties and obligations of the employer to the employee and *vice versa*, and the provisions of the contract form the basis on which the effectiveness of an organisation's current absence control policies should be assessed.

Contractual terms may be either express or implied. Express terms are those actually agreed by the parties and also include, if specifically agreed by the parties, collective agreements and works rules. Implied terms are those which may be inferred by the courts or tribunals if not expressly stated by the parties. Implied terms consist of the duties and obligations imposed on the parties by statute, custom and practice (as indicated by the past practices adopted by the parties) and common law. Terms implied by statute are fundamental and cannot be undermined. Thereafter, express terms take precedence over all other sources – ie terms implied by custom and practice and common law (Lewis, 1994). The terms of an employment contract do not have to be specified in writing, but there is a statutory obligation under the Employment Rights Act 1996 (which re-enacts the provisions of the Employment Protection Consolidation Act 1978, as amended by the Trade Union Reform and Employment Rights Act 1993) to issue written particulars of specified terms and conditions not later than two months after the commencement of continuous employment. There is no statutory requirement as such to provide written particulars of absence procedures or absence management policies. However, related requirements, quite apart from good practice, strongly suggest that an employer should do so in order to clarify exactly what standards are expected.

The statutory requirements related to absence management policies and procedures are listed below.

First, the written statement must include terms and conditions relating to incapacity for work due to sickness or injury, including any provision for sick pay. This does not imply that an employer must have an occupational sick pay scheme, since the only legal obligation is to pay statutory sick pay. If, however, an occupational sick pay scheme applies, details of it must be provided – and where it does not, the written particulars must say so. The details of any occupational sick pay scheme do not need to be set out in full in the written statement: it is sufficient to refer employees to a separate document which they have a reasonable opportunity of reading. Any changes to the current arrangements must also be notified in writing.

A second requirement impinging upon absence management relates to the statutory obligation to include particulars of any disciplinary rules and procedures applicable to employees, either in full or by reference to another document. Information should include the names or descriptions (eg job titles) of the people to whom employees can apply if dissatisfied with any disciplinary decision and how they should go about this. To the extent, therefore, that absence could become a disciplinary matter (as discussed below), statute requires that the disciplinary framework which would apply needs to be brought to employees' attention.

It will be evident from the above that two important issues are raised in relation to the employment contract and absence management. First and fundamentally, do our contractual provisions – including associated policies and procedures for absence management – comply with the relevant statutory framework and the ACAS Code of Practice on Disciplinary Practice and Procedures in Employment? Second, do the terms of our contract, whether expressly stated in each contract or specifically referred to by virtue of collective agreements, works rules or staff handbooks, provide a sufficiently clear and unambiguous framework for effective absence management? It is to these issues that we now turn.

The statutory framework and the ACAS Code of Practice

Under the Employment Rights Act (ERA) and the subsequent statutes referred to in the last section, eligible employees (in the main employees with two years' service) are entitled not to be unfairly dismissed. When determining unfair dismissal claims, tribunals consider two points:

☐ Has the employer established a potentially fair reason for dismissal?
☐ Did the employer act reasonably in all the circumstances and use proper procedures?

The ERA establishes the principle of 'potentially fair' reasons for dismissal, and two of these in particular are of concern when contemplating dismissal as a result of absence. In the case of long-term sickness absence, the potentially fair reason will usually be on grounds of the capability of the employee to perform the kind of work he or she was employed to do. 'Capability', according to the ERA, is assessed by reference to skill, aptitude, health or any other physical or mental quality, and 'the kind of work' as work which the employee could be required to do under the contract of employment, not just the kind of work actually being performed prior to the sickness absence (IRS, 1995a, p.3). The implication here is that employers are expected to take reasonable steps to find and offer suitable alternative employment either in advance of, but in any event following, an employee's return from sickness absence if appropriate in the light of the employee's state of health. In the case of persistent short-term absences, on the other hand, the potentially fair reasons for dismissal are likely to be either capability, where investigation has indicated some underlying medical condition, or misconduct where no medical explanation has been identified. In exceptional circumstances, the potentially fair reason may be 'some other substantial reason' (SOSR). In all circumstances, the onus of proof is on the employer to establish a potentially fair reason, and if that cannot be established the employer's case will fail.

The second issue which tribunals consider is whether the employer acted reasonably or unreasonably in all the circumstances and used proper procedures. When determining this, tribunals take into account 'the size and administrative resources of the employer's undertaking' and make a decision 'in accordance with equity and the substantial merits of the case'. Tribunals are not bound by precedent and may apply different standards to different employers, taking into account the size of the organisation and all the facts before them. In practice, reasonableness includes:

☐ use of proper procedures (as provided for in the ACAS Code on 'Disciplinary Practice and Procedures in Employment')

☐ the consistency of the employer's decision in the light of previous dismissals and disciplinary action

☐ the appropriateness of the dismissal penalty in the light of the offence, the length of service of the employee, his or her previous good record, and any other mitigating circumstances, such as domestic or personal difficulties.

In making their judgement, the tribunals may take the provisions of the ACAS Code into account, and employers who can demonstrate that they have complied with them will be better placed to demonstrate that they have acted reasonably. A useful preliminary step for organisations that wish to tackle absence in a manner which can be demonstrated as reasonable before a tribunal is to audit current disciplinary procedures in the light of the ACAS Code.

However, it is important to note that cases of genuine illness, as distinct from intermittent absences which cannot be explained on health grounds, should not be treated as disciplinary cases. According to the judgement of the Employment Appeal Tribunal (EAT) in the case of *Lynock v Cereal Packaging Ltd* (1988), genuine illness requires employers to treat each case with sympathy, understanding and compassion, whilst at the same time giving clear indications of the risks to the employee's continued employment should the sickness absence persist (IDS, 1994c, p.21). As indicated later in this chapter, the decisions of tribunals, together with further non-statutory guidance on handling absence contained in the ACAS handbook *Discipline at Work* (1988), require special procedures to be followed. In the case of longer-term sickness absence, relatively exhaustive processes of enquiry and investigation into the nature of the illness are required, its likely duration and its potential impact on the employee's future employment. Even in the case of persistent shorter spells of absence, although less burdensome, certain processes of investigation are nevertheless also required.

Express contractual terms and absence management

In addition to outlining an organisation's contractual procedures for handling absence, the express terms of the employment contract – whether specifically within each individual contract or in collective agreements, works rules or staff handbooks – must provide a sufficiently clear and unambiguous framework for absence management (as noted above). This section highlights a range of issues which have to be taken into account and documented as express terms of the employment contract.

Essentially, absence management – like all aspects of managing organisational discipline and performance standards – requires a 'control' process. This involves setting the desired standards and measures of performance required, monitoring against the standards set, taking corrective action, and providing follow-up feedback on performance after the corrective action has been taken. The absence control procedures of many organisations, where they exist, contain elements of this control process but are very often weak on the precise measures of the level of performance required.

The standards set in many organisations focus on *procedural* standards, such as a requirement to notify an absence on the first day by telephone and thereafter to produce the appropriate medical certificates at specified intervals. Many organisations monitor by keeping and disseminating absence statistics, and some also provide for a return-to-work interview, as discussed in previous chapters. Corrective action usually involves the use of the first stage of the disciplinary procedure or, in some cases, an absence counselling interview may be held in order to try to achieve some improvement prior to the commencement of formal disciplinary action.

What is lacking in this control process are precise measures of the performance standards required. The result is uncertainty and inconsistency. Many employees have no clear idea of what absence levels will or will not be tolerated, and managers have no clear yardsticks against which to judge what levels of absence constitute grounds for taking either informal or formal disciplinary action. A few organisations have attempted to tackle this by establishing precise measures of what constitute unacceptable or unsatisfactory absence rates and what disciplinary actions will follow from breaches of these standards, and have incorporated these rules as express terms of the employment contract. By setting such precise measures, employers leave staff in no doubt about the attendance standards expected, and help to ensure that absence control procedures are applied fairly and consistently by managers. These are sometimes referred to as 'absence triggers' and were described in Chapter 3.

When implementing a policy that relies on absence triggers, managements need to consider what scope there may be for a joint approach involving the trade unions – and such an approach lies at the heart of the recommendations of ACAS towards disciplinary rule-making. In their handbook on *Discipline at Work* (1988, p.8), it is recommended that 'management should aim to secure the involvement of employees and any recognised trade unions when disciplinary procedures are introduced or revised.'

These recommendations reflect its statutory code of practice on Disciplinary Practice and Procedures in Employment (1977, p.2) which, while recognising the possible reluctance of trade unions to become involved in the matter of disciplinary rules, makes the following proposals regarding the formulation of disciplinary rules and procedures:

> If they are to be fully effective, the rules and procedures need to be accepted as reasonable both by those who are to be covered by them and by those who operate them. Management should therefore aim to secure the involvement of employees and all levels of management when formulating new or revising existing rules and procedures. In the light of particular circumstances in different companies and industries trade union officials may or may not wish to participate in the formulation of the rules, but they should participate fully with management in agreeing the procedural arrangements which will apply to their members and in seeing that these arrangements are used consistently and fairly.

It is important if absence control is to be effective, therefore, that employment contracts contain rules about objectively measurable standards of attendance, as well as information about the procedural aspects of absence notification and monitoring. Where appropriate there should be employee and trade union involvement in agreeing the procedures to be followed and, where possible, in defining the measurable standards themselves. However, it must be stressed that a breach of attendance rules alone may not of itself be viewed by a tribunal as sole justification for dismissal. Tribunals have found dismissals to have been unfair where absence triggers have been applied too rigidly. Employers must still take account of all the surrounding circumstances and operate the rules established reasonably and with due regard for any mitigating factors in each individual case.

The doctrine of frustration and long-term sickness absence

Another issue which may arise out of long-term sickness absence is the question of whether the employment contract has become 'frustrated'. Frustration occurs where events outside the control of the parties make further performance of the contract impossible or radically different from what the parties originally intended. The effect of frustration is to bring to an end the existence of the contract and the obligations of the parties under it. For employees the effect of frustration is that they enjoy no employment protection rights – for example, rights to claim unfair dismissal – since the contract is no longer in existence, having been brought to an end by the process of law. IRS (1995a, p.2) has concluded that as a result of this loss of employment rights 'the tribunals and courts are reluctant to find that frustration has occurred' because of the potentially adverse effect on good industrial relations, and are unlikely to do so unless the employee has little prospect of recovery. It should also be noted that the burden of proof is on the employer to establish that the contract has been frustrated.

Key factors taken into account when determining whether frustration has occurred include the following, any of which may be considered in any assessment of the overall facts of the case (IDS, 1994c, pp.10–12, IRS; 1995a, pp.2–3):

☐ *The prospect of recovery.* This an important factor and it is unlikely that frustration will be found to have occurred unless the employer has gathered clear medical evidence that an employee has little prospect of recovery. The mere risk of a future deterioration in an employee's health is unlikely to provide sufficient evidence that frustration has occurred. Employers may also be expected to be patient in waiting for a recovery to occur. In the case of *Hebden v Forsey and Son*, an absence of nearly two years as a result of an eye operation was not found sufficient to frustrate the contract.

☐ *Length of service.* As will be described further below in the context of sickness absence dismissals, employers are generally expected to be more patient in awaiting the return of a longer-serving employee.

☐ *Expected future duration of employment* if sickness absence were not a factor. This takes into account the temporary or permanent nature of the employment and whether it was likely to have come to an end irrespective of the sickness absence.

☐ *The employer's need for the work to be done.* This factor focuses on the extent to which the absent employee's skills and knowledge are readily replaceable. If they can be replaced by another employee, the employer can be expected to wait longer than if the skills and knowledge cannot so readily be replaced and a new appointment becomes necessary. For example, in the case of *Hunt v A.R. Marshall and Sons*, a tribunal held that an employer could not be expected to continue with temporary arrangements after the absence of a key worker for four months.

☐ *The nature of the job.* Employers are expected to assess the potential impact of the illness on the employee's ability to perform the job or a reasonable alternative job in the future before frustration can be considered to have occurred.

☐ *The risk of that employer might acquire employment protection obligations towards a replacement employee.* In assessing whether a contract might be frustrated, employers are entitled to take into account redundancy or unfair dismissal rights that would accrue to replacement employees after the requisite period of service.

☐ *Whether the employee has gone on being paid.* Where an employer continues to pay wages or sick pay or to make continued payments to an employee's pension fund, it may constitute evidence that the employer wishes to maintain the contractual relationship. It should be noted, on the other hand, that the mere exhaustion of occupational sick pay entitlement will not of itself permit the employer to consider the contract at an end. Employers' practices with regard to occupational sick pay vary enormously, given that there is no obligation to pay more than statutory sick pay. Practices can vary from the provision of no occupational sick pay scheme, as is the case in nearly half of private sector employers (particularly smaller ones), to up to one year's pay in the case of some large employers (IDS, 1991, p.7; IDS, 1994b, p.9). The vicissitudes of employers' sick pay policies thus mean that exhaustion of entitlement provides no conclusive evidence of frustration.

☐ *The acts and statements of the employer in relation to the employment.* The nature of frustration is that the ending of the contract does not require a formal act of dismissal since the contract has come to an end by the process of law. In cases of frustration, the courts and tribunals may nevertheless be interested to understand why there was no formal dismissal.

In the final analysis, the courts and tribunals will weigh up whether a reasonable employer can be expected to wait any longer for the employee to return. However, as IDS (1994c, p.12) conclude, 'employers should be cautious in invoking the doctrine of frustration'. It is recommended that where it is invoked, employers should be prepared to plead an alternative defence – namely, that there was a dismissal for a potentially fair reason on the ground of the employee's incapability through long-term sickness. Such a defence requires a fair procedure for handling long-term sickness, and it is to this topic that we shall now turn.

Long-term sickness procedures

As we noted at the beginning of the chapter, the burden of proof lies with the employer to demonstrate that a dismissal arising out of long-term sickness is for a potentially fair reason – and in the case of genuine illness, this relates to the employee's capability to do the kind of work he or she was employed to do or any alternative work of a broadly similar nature he or she might reasonably be expected to do. As well as establishing a potentially fair reason for dismissal, employers must also demonstrate that they acted reasonably and applied a fair and proper procedure.

General guidance on this is contained in the ACAS code on Disciplinary Practice and Procedures in Employment. In the case of dismissals arising out of long-term absence, further guidance is available regarding the fair procedures which must be followed.

The first source of these is the ACAS handbook *Discipline at Work* (1988, pp.40–45), which presents an authoritative but non-statutory view. The non-statutory nature of the ACAS handbook was emphasised in the case of *British Coal Corporation v Bowers* (1994) when the EAT reminded tribunals that it did not have the legal status of a statutory code of practice (IRS, 1995a, p.4). The second source of guidance emanates from the decisions of the courts and tribunals in long-term sickness absence cases. In addition, all the factors noted above in relation to frustration will also be considered in assessing the reasonableness of the dismissal, taking into account all the relevant facts in the circumstances of each individual case.

The remainder of this section considers each of the recommendations made by the ACAS handbook regarding the handling of long-term absence, adding guidance where available from relevant cases. A fair procedure for handling the dismissal of long-term sick employees consists of three elements (IDS, 1994c, p.13):

☐ consultation with the employee
☐ medical investigation
☐ consideration, where appropriate, of alternative employment before dismissing.

In addition, two further issues that arise out of long-term sickness dismissals need to be taken into account, and these are:

☐ the impact of providing permanent health insurance
☐ the impact of the Disability Discrimination Act (1995).

Each of these will be considered in turn.

Consultation with the employee

The ACAS handbook (1988, p.42) provides the following advice:

> The employee should be contacted periodically during the period of sickness absence and in turn should maintain regular contact with the employer.
>
> The employee should be kept fully informed if employment is at risk.
>
> Where the employee's job can no longer be kept open and no suitable alternative work is available, the employee should be informed of the likelihood of dismissal.
>
> Where dismissal action is taken, the employee should be given the period of notice to which he or she is entitled and informed of any right of appeal.

It is important to note that this process involves genuine consultation and two-way communication in order to establish the true medical position. According to the EAT, consultation has two purposes: to ensure that the situation has been properly weighed up, balancing the employer's need for the work to be done against the employee's need for time to recover; and to ensure that steps are taken to establish the true medical position (IDS, 1994c, p.14).

It is also important that genuine illness is treated with sympathy and understanding, not as misconduct on the part of the employee. The EAT has stated that 'warnings' are generally inappropriate in these circumstances and could even be damaging to the employee's recovery. However, warnings might become appropriate in certain circumstances where an employee exacerbates the situation by refusing to follow medical advice. Examples here include refusing to follow a diet to control obesity or refusing to undergo a simple operation which would restore fitness for work. While warnings are generally inappropriate, except in such circumstances, the employer must nevertheless inform the employee if his or her continued employment is at risk, following the ACAS (1988) recommendations. The difference is one of nuance and emphasis and, as IRS have concluded (1995a, p.5), 'At the end of the day, tribunals will generally be more concerned with the procedures followed than with the labels given to those procedures.'

A failure to consult the employee is generally fatal to an

employer's case if dismissal action is taken. As Phillips J. stated in the case of *East Lindsey District Council v Daubney* (1977), 'If the employee is not consulted and given the opportunity to state his case, an injustice may be done' (IDS, 1994c, p.13). In this case the employers were found to have unfairly dismissed an employee on the basis of their own doctor's report, which in turn had been based on an examination carried out by another doctor. The employee had not been given an opportunity to state his case or to obtain an independent medical opinion.

According to IDS (1994c, p.14), proper consultation with the employee should include four specific points.

☐ Discussions should take place in the early stages of the illness and periodically throughout its duration, and the employer should give clear indications when the duration of the illness has begun to put the employee's future employment at risk. Following the recommendations of the ACAS handbook (1988), the employee should be informed when the decision to dismiss has been taken, should be given the period of notice to which he or she is entitled, and informed of any right of appeal.

☐ The employer should make personal contact before dismissal – ie the decision to dismiss must have been preceded by face-to-face contact and not have been conducted by post or on the telephone.

☐ The employer must give due consideration to the employee's opinions on his or her condition: this requires employers to take account of the employees' views on the likely date of return and about the work he or she would feel capable of performing on his or her return. However, employers must balance the employee's own assessment with that of professional medical opinion (as discussed below). The dismissal of an employee on the basis of a personal assessment of health alone is likely to be unfair. In the case of *Jones v Nightfreight (Holdings) Ltd* (1988), the employer relied on the employee's own assessment of the date when he thought he would be well enough to return, and when the employee failed to turn up on that date he was dismissed. The dismissal was found to be unfair on the grounds that the employer over-relied on the employee's own assessment at the expense of obtaining professional medical opinion (IDS, 1994c, p.15).

☐ The employer must give due consideration to possible alternative work, should the employee prove unable to return to his or her former duties. (This will be considered further below.)

There have been very few exceptions to the general principle that failure to consult is likely to render a dismissal for long-term sickness unfair (IDS, 1994c, pp.15–16). In the case of *Taylorplan Catering (Scotland) Ltd v McInally* (1980) the employee had suffered long-term sickness as a result of depression caused by working in an isolated environment in the Shetland Islands. The employee was subsequently dismissed without consultation. The employers took the view that consultation would have been pointless in that they could not alter the environment which had caused the illness. The EAT agreed, arguing that the purpose of consultation was to help an employee over the problem and get back to work – outcomes which were highly unlikely in this case. In another case, *Eclipse Blinds Ltd v Wright* (1992), the employee's health had deteriorated to a point which made return to work unlikely, a fact confirmed by her GP to the employer. Her GP had decided not to disclose her true medical condition and she believed she was getting better. In these circumstances, the employer dismissed without consultation for fear of disclosing the true position inadvertently, and the court held that the employer had not acted unreasonably in these specific circumstances.

Medical investigation

The general position is that employers must take steps to find out about the employee's true medical position, and that a failure to seek medical advice, where this is appropriate, is likely to result in a finding of unfair dismissal. The employer is therefore required to seek medical advice from an employee's GP or specialist, probably also from the company physician, if there is one, and sometimes to obtain the views of an independent specialist.

ACAS (1988, pp.42–43) summarises the steps which employers should take in order to obtain medical information about employees as follows:

Before applying to an employee's doctor for a medical report, the employer must notify the employee in writing that it is proposed to make the application and secure the employee's consent in writing.

In addition the employer must inform the individual that he or she has

- the right to withhold consent to the application's being made
- the right to state that he or she wishes to have access to the report
- rights concerning access to the report before (or after) it is supplied
- the right to withhold consent to the report's being supplied to the employer
- the right to request amendments to the report.

Where an employee states that he or she wishes to have access to the report, the employer must let the GP know this when making the application and at the same time let the employee know that the report has been requested.

A letter of enquiry [see ACAS, 1988], approved by the British Medical Association, may be used and the employee's permission should be attached to the letter.

The employee must contact the GP within 21 days of the date of the application to make arrangements to see the report; otherwise their rights will be lost.

If the employee considers the report to be incorrect, the employee may make a written request to the GP to make appropriate amendments.

If the GP refuses, the employee has the right to ask the GP to attach a statement to the report reflecting the employee's view on any matters of disagreement.

The employee may withhold consent to the report's being supplied to the employer.

On the basis of the GP's report the employer should consider whether alternative work is available.

Where there is reasonable doubt about the nature of the illness or the injury, the employee should be asked if he or she would agree to be examined by a doctor to be appointed by the company.

Where an employee refuses to co-operate in providing medical evidence or to undergo an independent medical examination, the employee should be told in writing that a decision will be taken on the basis of the information available and that it could result in dismissal.

Where an employee is allergic to a product used in the workplace, the employer should consider remedial action or a transfer to alternative work.

The 'rights' to which ACAS are referring emanate from the Access to Medical Reports Act (1988) and the Access to Health Records Act (1990). The Access to Medical Reports Act gives individuals some specifically defined rights in relation to medical reports relating to them which are supplied by medical practitioners for employment purposes. The Act defines a 'medical report' as a report prepared by medical practitioners responsible for the clinical care of the individual (IRS, 1995a, p.5). This definition is therefore likely to exclude reports prepared by company doctors or independent specialists who are not responsible for the clinical care of the individual.

The Act requires employers to notify employees of their wish to approach their personal physician for a medical report, to obtain the employee's consent to make the application, and to inform the employee of his or her rights under the Act. These rights include giving consent for the application to the personal physician to be made and for a report to be supplied; the right to see and agree the contents before it is supplied; and the right to request alterations or amendments before it is supplied. If the employee's physician does not accept the need for any proposed alterations or amendments, the employee has the right to append his or her comments before it is supplied. The employee's right of access to the report can only be limited or denied where a doctor believes that disclosure could be potentially damaging to the patient's physical or mental health. It is important to stress that the employee ultimately has the right to withhold consent for a medical report to be supplied, but any refusal to co-operate in this way has implications which are discussed below.

In terms of the procedure to be followed to obtain consent, employers should write to the employee seeking consent to approach the personal physician for a medical report, inform

Chartered Institute of Personnel and Development

Customer Satisfaction Survey

We would be grateful if you could spend a few minutes answering these questions and return the postcard to CIPD. <u>Please use a black pen to answer.</u> **If you would like to receive a free CIPD pen, please include your name and address.** IPD MEMBER Y/N

....

1. Title of book ....

2. Date of purchase: month ....   year ....

3. How did you acquire this book?
☐ Bookshop   ☐ Mail order   ☐ Exhibition   ☐ Gift   ☐ Bought from Author

4. If ordered by mail, how long did it take to arrive:
☐ 1 week   ☐ 2 weeks   ☐ more than 2 weeks

5. Name of shop .... Town....................................... Country ....

6. Please grade the following according to their influence on your purchasing decision with 1 as least influential: (please tick)

	1	2	3	4	5
Title					
Publisher					
Author					
Price					
Subject					
Cover					

7. On a scale of 1 to 5 (with 1 as poor & 5 as excellent) please give your impressions of the book in terms of: (please tick)

	1	2	3	4	5
Cover design					
Paper/print quality					
Good value for money					
General level of service					

8. Did you find the book:
Covers the subject in sufficient depth   ☐ Yes   ☐ No
Useful for your work   ☐ Yes   ☐ No

9. Are you using this book to help:
☐ In your work   ☐ Personal study   ☐ Both   ☐ Other (please state)

Please complete if you are using this as part of a course

10. Name of academic institution..

11. Name of course you are following? ....

12. Did you find this book relevant to the syllabus? ☐ Yes   ☐ No   ☐ Don't know

Thank you!

To receive regular information about CIPD books and resources call 020 8263 3387.

Any data or information provided to the CIPD for the purposes of membership and other Institute activities will be processed by means of a computer database or otherwise. You may, from time to time, receive business information relevant to your work from the Institute and its other activities. If you do not wish to receive such information please write to the CIPD, giving your full name, address and postcode. The Institute does not make its membership lists available to any outside organisation.

1795/05/00

2 1

Publishing Department

Chartered Institute of Personnel and Development

CIPD House

Camp Road

Wimbledon

London

SW19 4BR

the employee of his or her rights, and obtain written acknowledgement and agreement to all the contents of the letter. The next step is to write to the personal physician (see ACAS, 1988 for an example letter), attaching the employee's consent.

The Access to Health Records Act (1990), which came into force on 1 November 1991, gives individuals the right of access to 'health' records made by any health professional responsible for care after that date. The distinction between this and the 1988 Act is that the latter refers to 'reports' by a personal physician and the former to 'records' created by any health professional. Employers may, with the employee's consent, also obtain access to his or her medical records.

Some issues arise out of the cases and have implications for the application of the procedures recommended by ACAS.

The first point of contact is usually the employee's GP, who should be asked about the nature of the illness, the expected period of absence and the type of work the employee will be capable of on return to work, subject to the employee's consent to make such enquiries (IDS, 1994c, pp.16–17). In return, the employer should give the GP (or any specialist) information about the nature of the employee's work, the reasons for the enquiry and the risks (if any) to the employee's future employment (IRS, 1995a, p.6). Employers should not, however, rely solely on the diagnosis of the GP as stated on the medical certificate or in any report supplied or from any other correspondence. In the case of *Crampton v Dacorum Motors Ltd* (1975), the employer dismissed a service manager aged 50 on the basis of the GP's diagnosis of angina, having made some further informal enquiries about the nature of this condition. The dismissal was held to be unfair on the grounds that in such circumstances employers must take reasonable steps to discover all the relevant facts, which should have involved further examination by a specialist identified either by the employee's physician or by the company (IDS, 1994c, p.17; IRS, 1995a, pp.5–6).

A second issue may arise where employers have sought and obtained a second medical opinion – for example from their own company doctor – which differs from, say, that of the employee's GP or the specialist. If the employers decide to dismiss on the basis of one of these reports, they will need to show reasonable grounds for preferring one medical opinion over another. There are some indications from the cases that the views of employers' medical advisers may carry more weight because of their greater knowledge of the job and the working environment. This was the case in *Ford Motor Company v Nawaz* (1987), where the EAT held that employers could not be expected to weigh up conflicting medical opinion and had acted reasonably in dismissing on the basis of their own medical advisers' opinions (IRS, 1995, p.6).

Ultimately, as the EAT have stated, the decision to dismiss is not a medical question but an employment question, taken in the light of the available medical advice (IDS, 1994c, p.18). However, the employers may still run the risk that they have dismissed without a thorough investigation of all the facts. In the case of *British Gas plc v Breeze*, the opinion of the employers' medical adviser conflicted with that of the employee's GP, who held the view that the employee would be able to return to his job. The company's medical adviser recommended that a third, independent opinion should be sought, but this was not taken up. It was held that the dismissal was unfair on the grounds that more information should have been sought (*ibid*). So, while there appears to be some conflict between these decisions, employers may well be advised to obtain a third opinion where the first two opinions differ.

A third issue which may arise concerns an employee's refusal to consent to a medical examination or to the disclosure of a medical report or medical records. An employer cannot force an employee to undergo a medical examination, unless that has been provided for in the contract, and cannot in any event gain access to a medical report or medical records without the employee's consent. Provided that the employer has taken reasonable steps to secure the employee's co-operation in gathering medical evidence, but has failed to do so, the employer is then entitled to take action on the basis of the evidence available, even if that falls short of revealing the full medical position. This means that a dismissal may be held to be fair even if medical evidence, had it been available, might have indicated to the contrary (*ibid*). This was the position in the case of *McIntosh v John Brown Engineering* (1990), where a dismissal was found to be fair following an employee's refusal to allow a report to be given to the employer by his GP, or to be examined by a company doctor or by an independent specialist (IDS, 1994c, p.17). Employers must, however, have followed the consultative process described earlier and have taken all reasonable steps to obtain medical evidence.

Whatever the issues regarding medical evidence, the EAT has recognised that the decision to dismiss a long-term sick employee is not a medical but a management issue. According to IRS (1995a, p.6), the process of consulting the employee and medical opinion should provide sufficient information for the employer to provide answers to the following questions.

☐ Is the employee likely to make a full recovery, and if so, how long will it take? Can the employer reasonably be expected to keep the employee's job open until he or she is fit to return to work?

☐ If the employee is not going to recover completely, what will be the extent of his or her continuing disability? Will this affect the employee's ability to do the job which he or she was employed to do?

☐ If it is likely that the employee will only recover sufficiently to resume work in some different capacity, is it possible to offer some alternative employment on his or her return from sickness absence?

It is to this last question that we now turn.

Alternative employment

The ACAS handbook (1988, p.43) provides the following brief guidance:

> On the basis of the GP's report (or equally that of any other physician), the employer should consider, if appropriate, whether alternative work is available.
>
> The employer is not expected to create a special job for the employee concerned, nor to be a medical expert, but to take action on the basis of the medical evidence.

Evidence from tribunal and court cases strongly indicates that a failure to consider alternative employment properly, as distinct from considering it but finding nothing suitable, is likely to render a dismissal unfair. A number of cases illustrate the point. In *Dick v Boots the Chemists Ltd* (1991), the dismissal of a store detective after three years' absence was held by the EAT to have been unfair, even though a doctor's report stated that she would never be fit to perform her job again. The company's procedure had been seriously flawed by failing to consider alternative employment even in these circumstances (IDS, 1994c, p.23; IRS, 1995a, p.7). As IDS (1994c, p.24) have concluded, it is clear that seeking and, where possible, offering alternative employment is fundamental to a fair dismissal in long-term sickness cases.

Various decisions also indicate that an employer, though not expected to create a job, must take a flexible approach and consider what assistance might need to be provided in order to make a suitable offer of alternative employment. Decisions in various cases have included:

☐ a willingness to accept someone back on a part-time basis
☐ a willingness to accept someone on day work, even though the job is only performed in shifts
☐ a willingness to reorganise a job so that, for example, less heavy lifting is required
☐ a willingness to transfer an employee to other tasks – for example, where an allergy has prevented the performance of former ones.

The impact of providing permanent health insurance

A number of employers provide permanent health insurance (PHI) which makes payments to employees who suffer a breakdown in health that prevents them from continuing in their current or similar work. These payments are likely to continue until recovery, death or retirement, and some schemes require that the recipients of PHI benefit remain employees. Depending on the exact rules of the scheme, there will usually be some qualifying period of absence before any payments are made. The recent High Court case of *Aspden v Webbs Poultry and Meat (Holdings) Ltd* (1996) highlighted the care to be exercised by employers when dismissing a long-term sick employee with contractual rights to permanent health insurance. In this case, Aspden's contract entitled him to PHI after 26 weeks' incapacity, subject to his meeting the qualifying conditions, one of which was being an employee. The benefit was thus not available if he was dismissed. His employment contract also provided for dismissal on grounds of ill-health following three months on full pay and three months on half pay. In the event, Aspden was dismissed, losing his rights to PHI. The court decided that where there is a contractual right to PHI and the terms of the scheme require an applicant to be an employee, an employer cannot dismiss on health grounds – unless there are grounds for summary dismissal – and deprive an employee of these rights. The effect of this ruling is to make it difficult to dismiss an employee contractually covered by PHI where continued employment is a requirement of the scheme.

Olga Aiken has suggested that in such situations it would be sensible to replace an employee's original employment contract with a new one when he or she transfers to PHI for the sole purpose of paying the benefit or, alternatively, to agree with the insurer at the time of taking out the policy that employment can be terminated and the payment will be made direct by the insurer to the employee (Aiken, 1996a; 1996b).

The impact of the Disability Discrimination Act (1995)

The Disability Discrimination Act came into effect in December 1996 and embodies the rights of people who have 'a physical or mental impairment' which have a 'substantial' and 'long-term adverse effect' on the ability of an employee to carry out 'normal day-to-day activities' (CCH, 1997). A 'long-term effect' is one which has lasted at least 12 months or is expected to last that period. The Act protects an employee who is disabled within the above definition from discrimination in all aspects of employment, including recruitment, promotion, transfer, training and dismissal. Discrimination is defined as the treatment (by an employer) of a disabled person less favourably than others who are not disabled, without justification. It is also discriminatory for employers to fail to make 'reasonable adjustments' to either their premises or to their employment arrangements – such as working hours – where a failure to do so would cause a substantial disadvantage to a disabled person, subject to the resources available to the individual employer.

The key issues regarding the dismissal of a long-term sick employee who may fall within the definition of a disabled person for the purposes of the Act are as follows. First, even if an employee has not suffered 'impairment' for at least 12 months and not been absent for that period, he or she may be protected if medical opinion considers that it is likely to last that long. Second, it is important to bear in mind the definition of discrimination, as set out above. To discriminate, the employer must treat the employee 'less favourably' than others without a disability within the definition of the Act. It is essential, therefore, that employers treat all long-term sickness – cases, whether or not they could be defined as disabled under the Act – in the same way, and demonstrate that no one is treated more or less favourably. If this is done, long-term sickness dismissals should not be deemed unfair within the meaning of the Act. Third, however, employers need to bear in mind the obligation to make 'reasonable adjustments' to the workplace or working arrangements. It would, therefore, be discriminatory to refuse to implement such adjustments in order to allow a long-term sick employee who has recovered sufficiently to return to work. It would also be discriminatory to refuse to allow a return to work on the grounds that the employee is likely to lose too many days through absence. The only circumstances that permit less favourable treatment occur where the employee genuinely cannot do the job for which he or she was employed or any other job that might reasonably be offered, or where reasonable adjustments to the workplace are either impracticable or demonstrably beyond the resources available to the employer (*ibid*).

Procedures for dealing with persistent short-term absentees

While in many organisations longer-term sickness accounts for the majority of the time lost through all absence, persistent short-term absence for apparently unconnected reasons (such as colds, 'flu, headaches, etc) are difficult to plan for and disruptive to efficient operations. Both the ACAS handbook (1988) and various principles arising out of the case-precedents provide employers with further guidance on the procedures to be followed.

An essential starting-point is a full and proper investigation of the facts in order to try to establish the causes of the absences. If some underlying medical explanation is uncovered, the procedure for dealing with genuine sickness absence – as described above – should be followed. Ultimately, if there is no resolution to the sickness problem, any dismissal will be on grounds of capability. If, on the other hand, no medical explanation can be discovered, then any dismissal is likely to be on the grounds of misconduct arising out of the employee's poor attendance record. It is essential that employers on the basis of their investigation establish which of these two diagnoses is applicable, since the procedure to be followed – and the reason for dismissal – is different.

A further important point to note when tackling frequent short-term absences is the existence of clear rules and standards, as discussed above. However, as is always the situation when dismissing, the wider circumstances of each case must be taken into consideration. Such factors will include the employee's past attendance record, the existence of any mitigating personal or domestic problems, and the likelihood of the employee's attendance record improving in the future. So although the attendance rules may contain clear trigger points (as described in Chapter 3) for which certain disciplinary consequences have been specified, breach of these rules alone may not be sufficient to justify dismissal when the surrounding circumstances are taken into account.

The remainder of this section provides guidance on the procedures to be followed in the case of frequent and persistent short-term absenteeism.

The ACAS handbook (1988, pp.41–42) is a useful starting-point and recommends that the following processes should be followed:

☐ Absences should be investigated promptly, and the employee asked to give an explanation

☐ When there is no medical advice to support frequent self-certified absences, the employee should be asked to consult a doctor to establish whether medical treatment is necessary and whether the underlying reason for absence is work-related.

☐ If after investigation it appears that there were no good reasons for the absences, the matter should be dealt with under the disciplinary procedure.

☐ Where absences arise from temporary domestic problems, the employer in deciding appropriate action should consider whether an improvement in attendance is likely.

☐ In all cases the employee should be told what improvement in attendance is expected, and warned of the likely consequences if it does not happen.

☐ If there is no improvement, the employee's age, length of service, performance, the likelihood of a change in attendance, the availability of alternative work, and the effect of past and future absences on the business should all be taken into account in deciding appropriate action.

ACAS concludes its advice as follows (*ibid*, p.42):

> It is essential that the persistent absence is dealt with promptly, firmly and consistently in order to show both the employee concerned and other employees that absence is regarded as a serious matter and may result in dismissal. An examination of records will identify those employees who are regularly absent, and may show an absence pattern. In such cases employers should make sufficient enquiries to determine whether the absence is because of genuine illness or for other reasons.

The ACAS guidelines reflect good industrial relations practice, as does the guidance provided by the tribunals and the EAT. An important case was *International Sports Company Ltd v Thompson* (1980) in which the EAT elaborated on the procedures which employers ought to follow in cases of frequent short-term absence (IDS, 1994c, p.19; IDS, 1994a, p.9). The key steps identified are:

☐ a fair review by the employer of the employee's attendance record and reasons for the absences

☐ an opportunity for the employee to make representations
☐ appropriate warnings of dismissal if the situation does not improve.

The EAT concluded that if there was no adequate improvement in the attendance record after this procedure, dismissal would be justifiable (IDS, 1994c, p.20).

Each of the above steps will now be examined in turn.

The starting-point is the use of return-to-work interviews after each spell of absence, with brief notes taken during the discussions. If the pattern of short-term absences persists thereafter, there should be a further investigation of the individual's overall absence patterns, days lost and reasons given for each spell of absence. This requires the keeping of absence statistics and, ideally, a computerised system that automatically generates a report when specified absence triggers are passed or specified patterns are identified (eg patterns of Friday or Monday absences). In the case of a first offence, a meeting should be called with the employee to discuss the facts and seek more information. Depending on the procedure, such a meeting may in the first instance consist of an informal counselling discussion or it may form part of the formal disciplinary procedure. It is important that no assumptions or prejudgements are made about the nature of these absences, and the key priority must be to identify whether there might be an underlying medical explanation or whether other personal or domestic circumstances are causing the absences. In the case of frequent, short-term and apparently unconnected absences, the EAT has held that there is no absolute requirement to produce medical evidence or to contact the employee's GP, unlike the requirement applying to longer-term sickness absences.

Nevertheless, it would be wise for an employer to attempt to do so in order to demonstrate that reasonable attempts have been made to uncover some underlying explanation. For example, in the case of *Smith v Van Den Berghs and Jurgens Ltd* (1991) the employer was found to have unfairly dismissed an employee for misconduct due to his absenteeism for which no medical evidence had been sought. Medical evidence was subsequently presented to the tribunal by the employee and it was concluded that the absences were for genuine reasons (IDS, 1994c, p.20).

Where an employee's absences are mainly self-certificated, it would be appropriate for an employer to propose and seek an employee's consent to a medical examination. If an underlying medical explanation is uncovered, the procedures considered in the previous section for sickness absence should be followed. Equally, if the process of investigation and consultation reveals some personal or domestic problems, the employer should take note of them and the employee's views on how he or she is attempting to solve them. The employee should be allowed time to implement a proposed plan of action, and the situation should be kept under review.

Where no underlying medical explanation nor any other mitigating circumstances can be identified, continuing short-term absences should be dealt with through the disciplinary procedure. This will involve the use of warnings and possibly also the setting of attendance targets to be achieved. In the final analysis, an employer is entitled to conclude that 'enough is enough' and, having investigated the facts, explored the possibility of a medical or other explanation, consulted the employee regularly about the level of absence and followed the disciplinary procedure laid down, any ensuing dismissal is likely to be fair.

The key is establishing a fair reason on the basis of the facts and the discussions and acting by applying a fair procedure.

As well as considering the individual circumstances of the employee concerned, the employer is entitled to weigh up the impact of the absences on other staff and on the efficiency of the organisation as a whole. When dismissal is being contemplated, therefore, the EAT has suggested that employers need ultimately to consider the following factors which will be relevant to their tribunal evidence:

☐ the nature of any illness, if applicable

☐ the likelihood of any further absences recurring

☐ the length and frequency of the absences and the periods of attendance between them

☐ the need of the employer for the work to be done by a particular employee

- [ ] the impact of the absences on other employees
- [ ] the adoption and exercise of fair and consistent absence policies and procedures
- [ ] taking account of the employee's personal assessment in the ultimate decision
- [ ] the extent to which the difficulty of the situation and the position of the employer have been explained to the employee.

5

IMPLEMENTING AN ABSENCE CONTROL PROGRAMME

During the course of this book we have considered a number of perspectives on the management of absence: its measurement, its causes, its control and the importance of auditing organisational practices in the light of legal requirements. This last chapter is designed to provide the reader with a systematic framework for action within his or her own organisation. The implementation of an absence control programme will be considered in six stages:

1 Measuring and costing the current absence problem
2 Benchmarking and setting targets for achievement
3 Analysing the causes of absence
4 Analysing the effectiveness of current approaches to absence control
5 Planning and implementing an absence control programme
6 Monitoring and evaluating its effectiveness.

Measuring and costing the current absence problem

The availability of accurate information about absence levels in an organisation is a fundamental prerequisite of any effective programme of control. As described in Chapter 1, the key information required is time lost, frequency of absence instances, and absence costs. The need for such information may seem obvious, but it is surprising how many organisations do not collect it, according to various surveys of organisations' absence management practices.

According to the CBI (1993), around a third of organisations do not keep complete records of time lost by full-time staff, and even less information was gathered about part-time staff: only around a half of organisations surveyed kept information about part-timer absences.

The practices of organisations in relation to the analysis of information about absence costs is even more woeful. Only 24 per cent of respondents to the CBI's (1997) survey were able to provide an estimate of absence costs. A similar, but slightly more positive picture, was obtained by the Industrial Society (1997), but even here cost information could be provided by only around a third of respondents.

Evidence strongly suggests that many organisations fall at the first hurdle of any effective programme for absence control: they simply do not have the information. Without such information it is impossible to carry out external benchmarking of current performance, set targets for future performance or analyse costs. The latter is particularly worrying, since it implies that HR departments are unable to talk the language of costs, the 'lingua franca' of organisations. Moreover, the cost of absence will form the fundamental building-block of any absence control initiative. If HR departments are to persuade senior management of the need to invest resources in an absence control programme, any credible proposals will have to demonstrate what the current costs of absence are, what the likely costs of any absence control programme would be, and what cost benefits can be anticipated. Without such information it is unlikely that any proposals will be seriously entertained.

We have already noted that a considerable number of organisations do not have the raw data on absence from which to calculate costs, but even where the data are kept, many are still unable to cost it. A probable reason for lack of data about absence cost revolves around the time and difficulty involved in processing the data. According to the Industrial Society's (1997) survey of absence management practices, over a third of respondents said that absence was not costed because it would be too time-consuming, and nearly the same number said that they had no computerised personnel system to perform the calculations. No doubt these problems are interrelated. Clearly, gathering and costing absence data manually is very time-consuming. It is therefore suggested that, in all but the smallest organisations, some computerised system of absence recording and reporting is a prerequisite of any effective absence control programme. Where no computerised personnel system exists, an analysis of the costs of absence and of the potential for cost savings as a result of more effective monitoring through computerisation could more than justify the investment in a system. Even in an organisation of 500 people, the cost of absence could be of the order of £500,000 a year, not counting the indirect costs of overstaffing, temporary workers, overtime or disruptions to workflow (Evans, 1991). In their 1993 survey, the CBI found that organisations relying on manual record-keeping for absence control had 16 per cent higher absenteeism than organisations which kept computerised records.

Even where a computerised personnel system is in place, questions need to be asked about the flexibility and adequacy of the system for producing the data required. Where there is some computerised absence recording facility, it is usually capable of counting days lost by individual, grade, department or other variables, although some cannot calculate the frequency or number of absence spells. A number of systems have more difficulties when it comes to absence costing because they do not hold data on hours of work or average pay, which are often stored separately on payroll systems and links between the two systems may be unavailable. Moreover, good computer systems ought to be capable of providing an integrated absence warning system. Such a system, as was described in earlier chapters, can be programmed to generate warnings to system users or line managers when certain absence thresholds or triggers are exceeded, and help to ensure that the appropriate follow-up action takes place on a consistent basis.

In short, then, the fundamental building-block of an effective absence control programme is complete and accurate information. Effective absence reporting procedures ensure that each absence is accurately recorded in the first place and held on computer for the purpose of analysis. The computer system itself needs to be sufficiently flexible so that all the statistics required can be calculated, including time lost, frequency of absence spell and absence costs. Ideally, systems should also be able to generate warnings to help ensure that effective follow-up action is taken in every case.

Benchmarking and setting targets for achievement

Benchmarking best practice has now become widespread in British industry, practised by at least two thirds of organisations (Syrett, 1993). It is essentially concerned with making statistical comparisons of performance with other organisations and assessing whether the performance measures in a given organisation are better or worse. Where they are worse, benchmarking can be used to establish targets for achievement in the future.

Fowler (1997) suggests that effective benchmarking involves the following activities:

Identifying the performance improvement area to be studied in terms of measurable criteria in order to make comparisons with other organisations. In the case of absence, the relevant criteria require adequate data using the standardised measures discussed above – time lost, frequency and cost for each relevant employee category, eg manual or non-manual, occupational group, location, etc.

Choosing relevant organisations with which to make comparisons. Obvious sources of comparative data are the surveys conducted regularly by the CBI and the Industrial Society. However, it should be recognised that nationally gathered data of this kind have limitations. These surveys provide general absence data by industry sector, occupational group, geographical region and organisational size, but not all of these in a single analysis.

If, for example, we wished to benchmark absence rates of systems analysts and programmers in a software house in central London employing 1,000 people, the national surveys provide highly approximate information for benchmarking purposes. Moreover, the data provided are sometimes based on averages, whereas when benchmarking we may wish to identify the best performer or an upper quartile performer and not wish to content ourselves with performing at the industry average. In this context, it should be noted that the CBI absence survey does provide information on upper and lower quartile absences by industrial sector.

For more precise benchmarking information it is necessary to target organisations with whom we wish to compare ourselves. These may be competitors or organisations recognised as setting high standards of performance. Such an approach requires participation in benchmarking 'clubs', either run by consultancies or established on a voluntary basis by organisations.

Studying benchmarking data to identify possible opportunities for improvement. For example, if the data show that the average level of performance amongst competitors is a 6 per cent absence rate, but the best performer achieves 3 per cent, organisations ambitious for significant performance improvements might target themselves to match the best rather than the average performer. Benchmarking data therefore helps to establish targets for achievement.

However, when establishing such targets it is necessary to be realistic. First, benchmarking data must be gathered for comparable groups: the absence targets set for, say, senior managers, clerical staff and manual workers are likely to be different. Second, when setting targets for improvement it would be sensible to recognise that they cannot be achieved overnight. It is therefore worth taking on board the idea of continuous improvement, setting year-by-year targets to be achieved by departmental managers that bring absence levels down progressively over a period of time. Two of the case-studies which follow this chapter demonstrate that bringing absence rates down significantly can take a number of years.

Using benchmarking data to examine the procedures of the best-performing organisations in order to pick up ideas that can be adopted or adapted to achieve improvements. Benchmarking is very much concerned with performance measures, but it is about more than that. It also involves the sharing of information about what was done to achieve absence reductions, which policy initiatives worked, which did not, and what practical difficulties had to be overcome.

Benchmarking is concerned with establishing realistic targets for improvement. Data may be gathered from the regular national surveys or by participating in initiatives with other organisations. The results will be both measurable targets for achievement on a department-by-department basis and the generation of qualitative ideas about the content of any new absence reduction initiatives.

Analysing the causes of absence
Having gathered information about targets for achievement and a range of ideas worth further consideration, the next step is to analyse the nature of the organisation's absence problem so that any policy initiatives proposed are appropriate to the causes and sensitive to the organisation's culture. There is no point in introducing policies to tackle causes of absence that do not exist or grafting on ideas which worked elsewhere but would be unlikely to work in an organisation with a totally different cultural setting.

An analysis of the causes of absence can be achieved in a number of ways. First, absence records should be explored to identify what causes of absence have been given by employees. However, it needs to be recognised that though the effort is worth making, the value and reliability of the information may suffer from some limitations. It is certainly useful to identify what proportion of total absence can be accounted for by medically certificated longer-term sickness, as distinct from short self-certificated spells. It is also worth analysing absence by department, occupational group, grade or location to identify where the problems appear to lie, considering absence patterns (eg Monday or Friday absences), and it is important to find out the extent to which total absence can be accounted for by groups of individuals. In order to get behind the bare statistics, it is also useful to gather the views and opinions of supervisors and line managers and, where the organisational climate is felt to be appropriate, possibly the views of employees also.

In smaller organisations opinions can be gathered by means of face-to-face interviews, while in larger organisations a written questionnaire may be more appropriate. The latter has the advantage that it can be made anonymous and may therefore encourage more frank and honest replies than in face-to-face interviews. Careful thought must be given to the contents of interviews or questionnaires so that they explore the causes that are relevant to the circumstances of a given organisation.

The checklist set out below summarises a range of causes of absence drawn from the earlier chapters of the book, but not all will be relevant to every organisation. In order to refine the list to the factors which are relevant, small 'focus groups' of managers and supervisors (and, where felt appropriate, employees) can be organised to discuss the issue of absence, to present all the possible causes, and to give their assistance to refine the list to those issues which they believe are worthy of further exploration.

The next step is to design the questionnaire. While it need not require the name of the respondent if anonymity is thought helpful, it does need to seek some basic information in order to analyse the responses – for example, department and location. The form should also be designed so that respondents can provide analyses for different employee groups if a wide range of different occupational groups is represented in a department. Finally, the questionnaire ought to embody some method of measuring the strength of response. Respondents should thus be asked to rate each of the possible causes on a scale from, say, '1' (highly insignificant cause) to '6' (highly significant cause) for each employee category. Keeping an even number of ratings, such as six in the above example, avoids a middle rating which does not produce useful information, and forces respondents to rate causes as either significant or not.

The questionnaire may also seek an assessment of the effectiveness of the organisation's current absence control policies and get feedback on some of the new ideas for absence control identified in the benchmarking study. The reader is referred to the sections below for more guidance on these.

Three final points need to be made about launching a survey. First, it is essential that it is not launched until the entire absence control programme discussed in this section has been carefully considered and there is clear top management commitment to carry out this exploratory research. Second, it is important that the questionnaire is piloted amongst a small sample of respondents to ensure that it is intelligible, and modified, if necessary, in the light of this exercise. Third, despite the complexity of the issues to be explored in relation to absence, it needs to be recognised that the longer the questionnaire and the fewer the number of simple 'tick box' or 'circle score' type of questions, the more respondents will be put off and the lower will be the response rate, with consequences for the quality and representativeness of the data gathered. So the questionnaire must be as short and as simple as is practicable.

The following causes of absence, together with their implications for absence control, have been identified in this book, but it will be necessary to consider which of these causes are relevant in a given organisational setting when developing a questionnaire:

Personal characteristics of employees

- [ ] *Length of service*. Higher absence levels may be expected where length of service is shorter, with the implication that measures to tackle labour turnover need to be considered.
- [ ] *Age*. Older employees tend to suffer more sickness absence, with implications for health screening at recruitment and occupational health programmes.
- [ ] *Gender*. Younger females tend to have higher absence than males of equivalent ages, but consideration needs to be given to the potential influence of domestic or family responsibilities as an underlying cause and the extent to which child-care facilities or flexible employment policies might help to reduce this.
- [ ] *Education and career opportunities*. Higher educational qualifications and opportunities to pursue a career tend to result in lower absence levels, but the provision of education and training at the workplace, together with policies of internal promotion and opportunities to learn new skills, may be seen as part of an effective absence control programme.

☐ *Past absence patterns*. Past absence patterns have been shown to be useful indicators of future absence, so screening at recruitment and selection, including pre-employment health questionnaires and medicals, should be considered.

☐ *Family size*. Absence has been found to be linked to family size, but as noted above, child-care facilities and flexible employment policies are relevant here.

☐ *Employee attitudes, values, work orientations and commitment*. Employees' attitudes and commitment to their work vary: negative attitudes and low commitment are associated with higher absence. Much can be done by organisations to influence these factors, from careful screening at recruitment and selection to a wide range of initiatives to enhance commitment through employee communication, participation, involvement, job redesign and teamworking.

Job and organisational factors

☐ *Work design*. Absence can be related to lack of job satisfaction arising from routine and boring work. Initiatives to eliminate this influence through job redesign and teamworking may thus be a feature of an absence control programme.

☐ *Stress*. Work-related stress is increasingly being recognised as a significant cause of absence and has a number of underlying causes which organisations need to consider. One of these is poor working conditions. Another is an unsafe working environment. Another is boredom (and was considered in the previous paragraph). Further causes include work overload and job insecurity, worry over career and promotional prospects, workplace relationships, and of course stress may arise from sources outside the workplace. These represent a very wide range of issues which potentially ought to be considered in any absence control programme. Increasingly, such issues at the workplace are being tackled through occupational health initiatives, employee assistance programmes and counselling.

☐ *Organisation and work group size*. Absence levels tend to be higher the larger the organisation and the larger the size of the work group. Moves towards delayering and subdividing organisations into smaller business units or profit centres and establishing smaller, team-based work groups may have the effect of reversing the relationship between organisation size and absence.

☐ *Work group norms and cultures*. These are often embedded in the history and traditions of an organisation and reflect both the priority given by management to a particular issue, such as absence, and management's willingness and ability to enforce sanctions. Where absence has been given low priority and, by implication, to some extent tolerated, absence levels are likely to be high. Where managements have laid out clear rules of conduct and enforced them consistently and fairly, absence levels are likely to be lower. We also considered the role of peer group pressure in enforcing high standards of attendance. As noted above, the greater the tendency to devolve decision-making in organisations, empower teams to make more make decisions for themselves and equip them with multiple skills, the more peer pressure is likely to act to reduce absence levels.

☐ *Sick pay policies*. Relationships have been found between the establishment of occupational sick pay schemes and higher absence, a right to time off being seen in some instances almost as an 'entitlement'. Needless to say, we would not advocate the withdrawal of occupational sick pay schemes, but aspects of their operation may need consideration. One approach is to make payments subject to management discretion, entitlement being withheld where there is clear evidence of abuse. Another is to lengthen the period of service before entitlement commences. Another is to pay for the first few days of absence only after an absence has reached a certain length. For example, if an absence has to last three weeks before the first three days of absence are paid for, how many people will stretch a two-week absence to three weeks in order to earn this payment?

External factors

☐ *Economic and market conditions*. Absence may tend to rise in times of economic boom and fall in times of recession. During economic upturns, additional job opportunities are available and people are apparently less concerned about losing a job as a result of disciplinary sanctions. During economic downturns, people become more concerned about job security and are apparently less likely to take time off. Organisations need to be aware of these tendencies when interpreting their absence statistics and trends, and recognise that some rise in absence may occur in economic upturns, but this should not prevent them from applying absence control policies and sanctions in order to counter them.

☐ *Genuine illness*. It has been reckoned that this accounts for between a half and two thirds of all absence and is probably the most significant of all the causes of absence which we have considered. While organisations would not wish to encourage sick employees to come to work, it also needs to be recognised that stress, personal and emotional problems, smoking and alcohol abuse may be underlying causes of a significant proportion of sickness absence. Much can be done to tackle these issues, including pre-employment health questionnaires and medicals, policies on smoking at work and alcohol abuse, the promotion of better health awareness, programmes of 'flu vaccination, employee assistance programmes and counselling.

☐ *Family responsibilities*. It was noted that otherwise highly motivated employees may, from time to time, experience constraints in their ability to attend because of family or domestic responsibilities. These may include the illness of children or other family members, or a domestic crisis, such as burst water-pipes. Such problems may be more frequent than is often supposed. For example, managers in the CBI's (1997) survey rated family or domestic responsibilities as the second most significant cause of absence after colds and 'flu. Policies such as flexitime – which enables employees to build up additional leave entitlements by accruing banks of additional hours worked – and other flexible employment policies, such as a willingness to allow employees to transfer from full-time to part-time working, or to jobshare, or to work permanently from home, or to work at home occasionally, may help to reduce time lost for family or domestic reasons.

☐ *Travel difficulties.* Absence levels rise the longer the journey to work, when the weather is poor, or where traffic is particularly congested. These factors serve to create constraints on people's abilities to attend even if in normal circumstances they are motivated to do so. Screening at recruitment might usefully explore the nature of the journey a prospective employee will have to make. The provision of some company transport service may be appropriate, especially if the workplace is poorly served by public transport from the nearest station. Steps might also be taken to encourage some car-pooling arrangements. Moreover, some flexibility to work from home will enable employees unable to get to work because of adverse weather or industrial action on the public transport services to do so rather than appear in the absence statistics.

Analysing the effectiveness of current approaches to absence control

The previous section suggested that a survey of managers' and supervisors' views about the causes of absence might also usefully get their assessment of current absence control policies and seek their opinions on what further initiatives might be considered. The following is a checklist of questions against which to audit current absence control practices, and it also serves to offer ideas for approaches that might be considered in the future.

Absence policies, procedures and recording arrangements

☐ Do we have clear written policies setting the standards of attendance required?

☐ Do we have clear rules regarding the notification of absence on the first day and thereafter?

☐ Do we have clear disciplinary rules, possibly incorporating 'absence triggers', for dealing with absence?

☐ Are return-to-work interviews always required?

☐ Are return-to-work interviews always carried out? And what mechanism do we have for ensuring this (eg a form signed off and tracked by the HR department)?

☐ Are all medical certificates checked?

☐ Are all absences reported to the HR department or other central recording point?

☐ Is there a procedure for absence counselling? And are all managers/supervisors aware of when it must be initiated and how?

☐ Are there clear procedures for dealing with both short-term intermittent absences and long-term sicknesses?

☐ Have all managers/supervisors been trained in all these provisions, including the skills of return-to-work interviews and, if appropriate, absence counselling?

☐ Have all these requirements been clearly communicated to all employees through such means as written terms and conditions, employee handbooks, induction, briefing groups, noticeboards, etc?

☐ Can the HR department provide accurate statistics on both time lost and absence frequency?

☐ Can the HR department provide absence costings?

☐ Is our absence recording system computerised?

☐ If so, is our current system adequate for the job?

☐ Does our computerised system trigger warnings when action is needed regarding any individual absence (eg when a predefined threshold has been exceeded)?

☐ Have we carried out an exercise to compare or benchmark our absence performance against other organisations'?

☐ Have we, in the light of the benchmarking exercise, set targets for achievement by individual departments in relation to absence levels'?

☐ If so, are regular feedback reports provided to managers on the absence performance of their departments, with summaries to senior management?

☐ Have we considered publishing 'league tables' of absence levels against target for each department?

☐ Are both employees' attendance levels and managers' performance in relation to absence management assessed at an appraisal interview?

Recruitment, selection and induction

- ☐ Do we have a pre-employment health questionnaire?
- ☐ Do we conduct pre-employment health screening?
- ☐ Are the questions of general health and attendance in previous employments discussed at the interview?
- ☐ Are potential travel-to-work problems discussed at the interview?
- ☐ Are references checked so that information on absence or attendance is collected?
- ☐ Does our employment contract clearly spell out the employee's obligations regarding regular attendance, the procedures to be followed and the disciplinary consequences of unacceptable absence levels?
- ☐ Are all these obligations reinforced at induction?

Rewards and incentives

- ☐ Have we considered the potential impact of occupational sick pay on absence? For example, is there any expectation that sick leave is an entitlement?
- ☐ Does our sick pay scheme provide flexibility for management to withhold it in cases of suspected malingering?
- ☐ Does our sick pay scheme encourage longer than necessary absences – for example, by paying for the first few days of absence after a certain length of absence has been exceeded?
- ☐ Have we considered the payment of attendance bonuses – eg cash bonuses – or 'prizes' for full attendance over a week, month, or longer period?
- ☐ Have we considered whether a group attendance bonus paid on a team basis might encourage peer pressure to attend?
- ☐ Have we considered 'plant-wide' schemes, based on the overall absence performance of a plant or location over a period of time or using absence as one factor in such schemes?
- ☐ Is absence included in any assessment of individual performance-related pay?
- ☐ Has an employee's absence record been considered for inclusion in the organisation's selection criteria for redundancy?

Work organisation and job design

☐ To what extent is absence the result of routine jobs and low levels of job satisfaction?

☐ Have we considered what might be done to reduce or eliminate our requirement for highly routine jobs, or investigated what might be done to provide more job variety through job rotation or broadening the range of tasks in a given job?

☐ What scope is there for enhancing employee involvement in job-related decision-making and providing more empowerment?

☐ Could we restructure or decentralise the organisation so as to create more employee identity with a sub-unit of activity?

☐ What scope is there for introducing teamworking, allied to multiskilling and greater mutual interdependence of roles, enhancing attendance motivation through commitment to the team?

☐ What scope is there to enhance commitment and motivation to attend through training and development, providing more opportunities to learn new skills or offering career development opportunities through internal promotion?

Flexible employment policies

☐ To what extent is absence the result of conflict between work and non-work responsibilities or a requirement for a more flexible lifestyle?

☐ Has flexitime been considered?

☐ How flexible are we in permitting full-timers to transfer to part-time work or to jobsharing in order that they can accommodate other non-work responsibilities?

☐ How flexible are we in permitting a pattern of daily hours of work which differs from standard hours so that employees can accommodate other responsibilities?

☐ Have we considered permitting home working or 'teleworking' on a permanent basis?

☐ Have we considered providing more flexibility to allow employees to work from home occasionally?

Occupational health initiatives

☐ To what extent is there a problem of genuine illness in the organisation?

☐ What is done to screen employee health at recruitment?

☐ Is there any evidence of stress?

☐ Are the working conditions and environment poor and in need of improvement?

☐ Are employees being overloaded with work?

☐ Have we trained managers in counselling skills to help employees with problems?

☐ Have we considered an employee assistance and counselling programme?

☐ Do we have 'no smoking' policies and do we do enough to help people give up the habit?

☐ What have we done about alcohol and drugs awareness?

☐ Have we encouraged greater employee fitness through subscriptions to gym, work-out or sports facilities?

Planning and implementing an absence control programme

As a result of working through the above analyses, we should now have a clearer picture of the nature of absence in our organisation, what works more and what works less effectively, and what new proposals are worth considering in the light of the cultural context of our organisation. The next step is likely to be a report on our findings, with a full review of the current levels and costs of absence, information gathered from the benchmarking exercise, targets which are felt to be achievable, the policies which are felt to be worth considering, the costs of the policy proposals themselves, and the cost savings and other benefits which are anticipated from the implementation of the proposed new initiatives.

The findings need to be considered by senior management since, without wholehearted top management commitment, which in turn will affect line management commitment, any initiative is unlikely to be successful. With such commitment it will then be possible to plan the implementation.

A variety of prescriptions are available for managing the implementation of new policy initiatives. Lewin (1951) sees the achievement of change in terms of 'unfreezing' the status quo, achieving movement to a new situation, and then 'refreezing'. Movement from the status quo will be encouraged by what he terms 'driving forces', but at the same time will be held back by 'restraining forces' and resistance to change. The task of management is to build on the driving forces and respond to the concerns which may lead to resistance. The main ways in which this can be achieved is through consultation and communication. In order to emphasise the driving forces underlying the absence control programme, management must communicate a vision of the potential benefits to employees of a new approach. It makes sense to devise a strategy that seeks to balance general tightening up of reporting requirements and disciplinary sanctions with some positive initiatives that may appeal to employees: carrots as well as sticks are necessary. Depending on exactly what is being proposed, such benefits may include

☐ cost savings leading to greater competitiveness and potentially greater job security
☐ less disruption to daily work routines as a result of less absence
☐ more opportunities for participation as a result of job redesign or teamworking initiatives
☐ opportunities to earn attendance bonuses
☐ provision of new facilities promoting employee health and welfare
☐ new opportunities for flexible working.

Some of the restraining influences that may emerge from an absence control programme include

☐ resistance from employees or their trade unions on the grounds that more employees will be disciplined, possibly for absences beyond their control or simply failing to turn up when ill
☐ resistance from line managers and supervisors who may feel

that on top of their many burdens they are now being required to allocate time for return-to-work interviews, to acquire new skills in absence counselling for which they may feel ill-equipped, or to complete more paperwork.

Potential employee and trade union resistance emphasises the importance of involving them in consultations over the reasons for the change and offering assurances that all staff will be treated fairly and consistently, as well as emphasising the benefits considered above. Similarly, managers need to be involved in the development of the initiatives, their concerns taken on board and the benefits of the proposals emphasised – for example, less disruption to the work of their departments through less time spent reorganising or rescheduling work because of absence.

Beckard (1992) puts forward the following ideas for consideration when managing change.

Obtain commitment from the top. The vital importance of top management commitment has already been referred to and this will be strengthened by having the chief executive's personal support. The commitment of all the members of the top management team also generates powerful signals to line managers about what the organisation believes is important and helps to gain their commitment.

Supply a written description of the changes. Proposed changes need to be documented. This may take the form of a policy statement or a more detailed briefing for management outlining the new proposals for absence management. A standardised briefing paper will be important so that all managers communicate the same information to staff. It may also be useful to append some possible questions and answers for the guidance of management in responding to staff questions.

Supply clear reasons for changing the status quo. Following on from the discussion above about 'driving forces', managers should also be briefed on the need for change and its potential benefits.

Gain widespread support. The significance of top management support in this has been noted, and the new absence control initiative might usefully be launched at a briefing of all managers, providing a clear explanation of the changes, what will happen when, what their roles will be, and what training will be provided for them and for staff generally.

Manage resistance. We noted above that there may be a tendency to resist something which is new and different, on the part of both managers and employees. The keys to managing this are education, communication and discussion so that views are aired and potential problems taken on board at pre-launch briefings of managers, with a willingness to change any of the proposals where genuine difficulties have been raised. As described earlier, trade unions should be consulted, where applicable, and again a willingness to take on board concerns should be demonstrated.

Monitoring and evaluating effectiveness

The important points to bear in mind here are

☐ Establish measurable criteria for evaluation – for example, targeted levels of absence for each department, occupational group or location.

☐ Monitor performance against the criteria by providing regular feedback reports to line management, with summaries for senior management.

☐ Ensure that any checks or controls built into the system, such as absence reporting forms, are working effectively.

☐ Ensure that any training planned has occurred, and evaluate the effectiveness of that training.

☐ Consider ways in which feedback on performance can be provided more generally, such as at departmental briefing groups, through in-house journals or via noticeboards.

☐ Carry out a major review of the programme after one year of operation, in consultation with line managers; receive feedback; make any adjustments as appropriate; and set new targets.

Conclusion

In the course of this book, we have considered absence from a variety of perspectives, in particular its measurement and costing, its causes, methods of control, the legal perspective, and the implementation of policy initiatives. The current level of absence need not be accepted as an inevitable fact of organisational life. Of course people will become ill, but the wide variations in absence levels experienced by different organisations, even within the same industry, cannot be explained simply by illness. Except in certain exceptional industries, good or bad employee health must be assumed to be normally distributed amongst different employee populations. As stated in our introduction, a major source of the difference must comprise the actions taken by the managements of organisations. In the field of absence management, as in many others, the HR practitioner has a major contribution to make. The key to a professional approach involves benchmarking best practice, aiming to match performance with the best rather than being content with matching the average, setting targets for achievement and monitoring to check that they are being met, taking on board the idea of continuous improvement by setting progressively higher targets and, above all, balancing a punishment-centred approach based on necessary rules and sanctions with positive incentives that are aimed at actively promoting attendance motivation.

APPENDIX:
CASE-STUDIES

Introduction

In this section we outline the experiences of three organisations in trying to tackle what were initially quite high absence
levels. The organisations have a variety of backgrounds: Iveco
Ford Trucks is manufacturing, and Royal Mail and Lewisham
Council operate within the service sector. In two cases policies
have focused on manual worker absence; in the third the
problem was concentrated in staff areas. They have also
adopted distinctly different policy prescriptions, but between
them cover the majority of policy options outlined in this book.

As to why they decided to tackle absence, there is a remark-
able similarity of objectives. First, absence was expensive. The
direct cost of absence at Royal Mail amounted to £11 million
per annum. Iveco Ford was required to part-fund the company
sick pay scheme but had no influence on payouts. Second,
absence also made it difficult to plan schedules when a
substantial part of the workforce – one in six at Lewisham, for
example – could be almost guaranteed to be away sick each day.
Third, high absence and management's failure hitherto to
tackle the problem gave the wrong messages about (a) the
culture of the organisation, and (b) management's willingness
to manage. Finally, tackling absence commonly formed a part
of other policies aimed at increasing flexibility, often underpinned by moves to harmonise terms and conditions between
blue- and white-collar workers.

Some key points are as follows.

All these policies have been refined over time in the light of experience and feedback both from managers and employees. In some cases the policies have been introduced deliberately around transitional arrangements; in others refinement has been more incremental and less structured. Constant change is often necessary because, although policies can have an immediate effect in reducing absence, experience shows that further reductions and/or maintaining improvements once the initial excitement has worn off need a regular reassessment of policies.

Management commitment is clearly crucial to successful absence management. Senior management *must* want to improve performance, and junior managers *must* equally be willing to implement policies. Transferring the enthusiasm of the personnel department for tackling absence to busy line managers is not always easy. Designing a policy and letting line managers get on with it isn't enough, and the case-studies underline the effort that goes into communicating the policy, and providing guidelines and training on implementing it. Another important feature of the case-studies is the effort made to involve employees in the process of tackling absence. All of the case-studies to some degree worked with trade unions to design and implement their policies.

Again to varying degrees the case-studies have not just set about tackling the problem: they have also looked to minimise the causes of absence. That can involve the provision of health and safety policies covering stress management, counselling and policies for dealing with long-term sickness; the introduction of a comprehensive and effective referral system; and the creation of a safe working environment to avoid accidents at work.

Although their approaches are different, the case-studies share one common feature: for them their particular mix of policies has worked and absence levels have been impressively reduced.

Case Study 1

Iveco Ford Trucks

Iveco Ford Trucks was established in 1986 as a joint venture between Ford and Fiat to manufacture trucks at Langley in Buckinghamshire. From the start the workforce had been covered by the Ford sick pay scheme and was jointly funded by contributions from the company and employees. Management saw a number of problems attributable to this scheme:

- a progressive increase in sickness absence rates amongst manual workers, which reached annual rates of 7 per cent
- an inability to plan production schedules effectively
- significantly higher Monday and Friday labour shortages than on other days
- although the company was a joint funder of the scheme it had no influence on payouts
- there were no effective control mechanisms to tackle abuses.

The unions were warned continuously about the problems of absence when management provided figures showing rates steadily rising. Equally important was evidence that sickness was increasingly a cause of overall absence.

Working arrangements did include back-up cover, but the company found that moving employees around had an adverse effect on product quality – particularly as it happened very often. Although the cost of cover was clearly an issue, the company's primary concern was the cost of absence in terms of its effect on quality and competitiveness. The opportunity arose fundamentally to deal with the problem when Ford abandoned its long-standing scheme and Iveco established its own arrangements.

The company set out to find an alternative based on full co-operation with employees and their trade unions. Union involvement in designing both the new scheme and an absence management strategy was comparatively easy to get: information on the extent of the problem had already been shared with them; the unions knew that if they wanted to influence the new scheme they had to be involved at the design stage; and the unions themselves were receiving complaints from members about the pressures on them to cover for absent colleagues. A joint working party was set up composed of personnel specialists, line managers, full-time union officials and shop stewards, who held structured discussions focusing on the joint benefits of improvement and the penalties of failure for both sides.

As fundamental principles, the working party agreed that the new scheme should aim to reduce the need to move labour to provide cover (employees did not, in any event, like being moved away from their normal work group), to reduce the manual absence level down to the then existing 3.5 per cent rate of salaried staff; and possibly at some future date to harmonise the sick pay arrangements of both sets of employees.

The key features of the new scheme were:

☐ no payment for the first three days of sickness for any employee if sickness for the whole plant exceeded 3.5 per cent in the previous six months (later reduced to the previous quarter)
☐ transitional arrangements to ensure a progressive reduction in sickness absence
☐ generous benefit levels
☐ individual attendance criteria.

The scheme was originally introduced for a four-month period, with days two and three of sickness (but not the first day) paid. After that, the transitional arrangements meant that for a six-month period day one was paid if absence in the previous six months was at or below 3.5 per cent, and days two and three were paid if the absence rate was 4.5 per cent or less. The target figure of an absence rate of 3.5 per cent or less also for days two and three was introduced in two stages.

Provided the 3.5 per cent target is met, the scheme offers generous benefit levels of full basic pay for two years from the first day of absence for proven cases of sickness. Besides the plant-wide criterion there are individual attendance criteria and no payment is made to employees if their individual record shows they have been absent sick on two or more occasions for a total of 20 days in the previous 12 months.

The company believes that the new scheme has brought a number of direct benefits.

☐ Absence levels have improved. From the 7 per cent rates under the old scheme, absence fell steadily to be just below the 3.5 per cent target in both 1993 and 1994. Although it has risen to marginally over 4 per cent since then, the absence rate remains well below the industry average, which is around 5 per cent.
☐ Sick pay costs have been reduced because the scheme does not pay out unless the targets are met.
☐ Lower absence means less movement of labour, thus improving quality and morale.
☐ The earnings of sick employees are protected.
☐ It has led to increased co-operation between the company and unions.
☐ Employees themselves 'own' the system and exert peer group pressure to reduce plant absence
☐ The new scheme has supported, and been supported by, the recent introduction of absence counselling programmes aimed at addressing the high level of frequent unrelated absences amongst some employees.

In addition there has been a major indirect benefit in the creation of a more positive culture of communication which has fed into the setting up of briefing groups, joint working parties on a range of issues, and the use of employee attitude surveys.

A disappointment, however, is that while there was a rapid improvement in absence levels over the early years of the scheme, recent moves to an absence rate below 3.5 per cent have not been achieved consistently. What the company calls 'an interesting phenomenon' is that in 1995 and 1996 absence would fall during those quarters when, because the previous quarter's rate had been above target, the first three days of sickness were unpaid, only to rise again when the target had been again met and the first three days were paid. In those two years the absence rate tended to move between 3.5 per cent and 5 per cent, typically over a two- to three-quarter cycle. The company suggests that one answer to this might be to use two individual targets to determine an employee's entitlement rather than one individual and one plant-wide target.

Case Study 2

London Borough of Lewisham

The London Borough of Lewisham is situated in south-east London. It employs 10,000 people evenly divided between teachers, manual employees, and officers. In 1988, average absence in Lewisham was just over 19 days lost per employee per year – over twice the national average level. Absence levels were highest in the 'caring professions'.

In 1990 when the Council set about reducing sickness absence levels, its first two steps were to find out more about the absence it had, where it was and what it looked like; and also to look at what other organisations had done. This latter was probably the most useful tool at that stage. The research pointed to a three-pronged approach to absence control based at strategic, departmental and individual levels, all underpinned by the fundamental view that line managers were the people best placed to deal with absence issues.

At the strategic level, Council members, chief officers, and personnel professionals set a corporate absence target of nine days (3 per cent). The personnel department were to produce biannual monitoring reports covering, for example, comparable levels of absence for departments and different levels of staff, and a breakdown of long- and short-term sickness. Strategic action also included the introduction of a computerised absence management system, a review of the occupational health service, the introduction of a training programme for managers, and the production of corporate management guidelines on dealing with absence.

At the next level, and operating within the corporate guidelines, senior managers and management teams within departments were empowered to set their own targets, with a view to each department's progressing at its own pace (smaller departments were expected to progress faster than large departments, for example), backed up by performance targets sometimes related to budgets. Managers were also able to develop their own action plans for dealing with absence: for example, one department now sends out letters of appreciation to staff who have taken no sickness leave during the year. Individual departments were made responsible for preparing quarterly absence reports comparing levels on a divisional and sectional basis. (The Council now notes as a good sign the fact that absence rates rise briefly once new reporting procedures are installed – this shows that levels are being reported properly.)

In keeping with the Council's policy of devolving responsibility down to the line, line managers and supervisors are expected to

☐ carry out return-to-work interviews *in every case* when someone is absent

☐ carry out a formal review after three separate incidences of absence in a three-month period

☐ ensure that employees are aware of Council policy on absence and follow absence report procedures

☐ ensure a disciplined attitude to unauthorised absence

☐ keep accurate attendance records.

The trade unions were involved from the beginning. They initially objected to the idea that managers should be questioning staff about their illnesses, and were concerned that individual staff might be unfairly treated. They also fundamentally differed from management in seeing the occupational health service as a welfare, rather than a management, service. In the event, however, threats of non-co-operation did not materialise.

The initiative started in 1990. In 1991 the average absence rate had fallen to 16.9 days (7.5 per cent), and by 1993 was down to 12 days (5.3 per cent). But then it started to level out, and there was still substantial variation by department. A particular problem was found in the social services department, particularly in elderly people's homes, where absence levels were well above the department and Council averages. While the Council average then was 12 days, in social services it was 21.4 days, and in elderly people's homes it was over 26 days per year.

A review showed that managers were not carrying out return-to-work interviews nor talking to staff about what constituted an 'acceptable level of absence'. A first step was to brief managers and to incorporate the necessary action to be taken into their performance objectives. A new initiative was also taken based on 'kickstarting' the process by carrying out a pilot of 100 return-to-work interviews in which managers were initially assisted by a specially appointed personnel officer, leading to the implementation of return-to-work interviews in all cases, and other follow-up interviews and letters.

Within six months absence had fallen to 15 days, but it has stuck at that level.

Lewisham felt that three particular approaches had contributed to the overall improvement in attendance, which on their own might not be enough to get absence down to the target rate, but nevertheless contained important lessons. These were:

- □ management action and guidelines
- □ training
- □ occupational health measures in relation to long-term sickness.

The *management action and guidelines* were central to getting over the message that the responsibility for taking action on attendance lay with line managers, and that this called for continuous and co-ordinated effort (including the provision of help and counselling to people who needed it). Senior management also emphasised that line managers had the key roles of influencing employee behaviour and performance, and creating an 'attendance ethos'. Consistent communication was of the utmost importance.

Even so, once the guidelines had been produced and issued, senior management remained unconvinced that managers had the skills and willingness to counsel employees about their absence; that they understood their right to take progressive disciplinary action where absence was more a matter of 'conduct' than 'ill-health'; and that they had moved away from the prevailing view that absence was not their problem – the 'if someone is sick, they are sick' attitude.

Changing the culture required a large investment in actual *training*. About 1,800 managers have some form of responsibility for staff. In the first 18 months of the programme the Council targeted about 1,000 managers to attend a one-day training and briefing programme. The other managers were targeted separately, but using the same programme, by the personnel departments in their own departments.

The programme focused on

- the occupational, medical and behavioural reasons why people might stay away from work
- methods of controlling absence focusing on people-based, work-based, and organisation-based approaches
- line managers' responsibilities and what the Council expected from its managers
- the role of the manager as counsellor.

The Council also carried out a review of its *occupational health* arrangements. This actually started more by accident than design! Originally the personnel department had wanted to do more about health promotion, but managers had emphasised the need for a better service on sickness referrals to the occupational physician. What became clear from research carried out by the personnel department was that managers used referrals as a means of shying away from tackling long- and short-term absence managerially. As a result the decision was taken to appoint King's College Hospital on a contract which comprised conducting 600 referrals a year, amongst other functions.

Generally, across the Council the rate of progress to the target rate suggested that further action would be needed to change the attitudes of employees and managers – the issue of what was an acceptable level of absence was still felt not to be getting through. Constant effort was required to reinforce the message that the organisation was serious about managing attendance.

In 1993, as part of a new initiative, the focus moved to getting management to motivate staff to attend work by creating a good employment atmosphere. They were also encouraged to manage – show an interest in – the whole person. Only once this environment existed should managers impose penalties for poor attendance. However, this was also the period in which managers started to consider dismissal as an option because of high absence levels.

By 1995, days lost to sickness absence had fallen to 10, and for 1996 they were close to the CBI national average of 8.4 days. Even so, further initiatives have been taken, involving

☐ more specific targeting of absence control linked to performance management and capability

☐ improved measurement and reporting systems, with feedback to line managers

☐ improved communication processes to spell out the council's policies on absence

☐ targeted consultancy work in areas of comparatively high absence focusing on management's actions in managing absence

☐ surveys looking at employees' attitudes and why they stay away from work

☐ better stress management

☐ a new training initiative, including a video training pack for managers.

The main lessons that Lewisham says it has learned are that a strategy to tackle high absence levels needs to be aimed at all levels in the organisation: senior managers and board level, managers with day-to-day line responsibilities, and employees themselves. Secondly, a sophisticated system of management information needs to be developed. Thirdly, the respective roles of line managers on one hand, and of personnel/occupational health professionals, on the other, need to be clearly defined. Finally, the chosen approach needs to be kept under constant review and be capable of adaptation to changing circumstances.

Case Study 3

Royal Mail Scotland and Northern Ireland

Royal Mail Scotland and Northern Ireland covers a vast area comprising two countries with 38 per cent of the UK landmass (including 68 islands) but only 12 per cent of its population. Over 1,800 million letters are delivered each year to 2.9 million delivery points. There are about 12½ thousand post-boxes, and over 1,300 million letters are posted. To provide these services the organisation employs 17,100 people.

In broad terms, benchmarking information shows that the Royal Mail has higher absence rates than many industries and compared to local government. In 1996 the sickness absence rate for the organisation was 4.3 per cent, some way above the whole UK figure (3.7 per cent). However, on a regional basis the rate compares favourably with the 'all Scottish industries' rate of 4.5 per cent. In terms of days lost to sickness absence, the Royal Mail lost an average of 14.6 days in 1996 compared to a UK public sector average of 9.3 days. This may in part be explained by Royal Mail's high percentage of manual workers in its workforce. While manual worker absence, both for full- and part-timers, was some 2 to 3 days above the public sector average, and 6 to 7 days above that of the private sector, there were signs that, although the 1996–97 overall figure was 4.9 per cent, the most recent six months (excluding January 1997) were showing a year-on-year reduction. Worryingly, there were also signs of a rise in the rate in some white-collar occupations (eg administration) where the absence rate in 1996 was 4.2 per cent.

The organisation's absence rate of 4.3 per cent was esti-mated to have a direct cost of just over £11 million per year. But there were also clear, but unquantifiable, indirect costs from reduced quality of service and customer satisfaction.

Analysis of absence pointed up three particular features. Days lost varied by the month, with modest peaks in July and October and a larger peak in January. December, on the other hand, tends to be a very low absence month. The December/January cycle may be explained by the high levels of overtime available prior to Christmas, which would encourage attendance, with a 'trade-off' occurring in January. The second feature was the big variation in absence levels across the organisation: absence rates in Inverness, for example, were below 3 per cent for both operational and administrative staff, whereas in Glasgow they were over 5 per cent in both cases, and in Edinburgh over 6 per cent for operational staff. Finally, unlike the national survey evidence, the Post Office experience is that absence rates are lower for temporary and part-time staff than for full-timers: the absence rate for temporary staff (who do receive sick pay) was nearly half that of full-timers, and that of part-timers was about half of 1 cent lower.

The bulk of absence is short-term – ie, less than 14 days in duration. The major cause in 1995 was musculo-skeletal problems. As a percentage of total absence the incidence of this particular cause has fallen recently as the organisation has started to pay for injured staff to visit a physiotherapist. Over the last three years, days lost from accidents at work has fallen from 10 per cent to 6 per cent of total absence due to policy efforts to achieve a better focus on health and safety at work.

In tackling absence, the organisation has seen a clear link between the achievement of Royal Mail's performance measures and employee satisfaction. Those parts of the Royal Mail nationally in the top 20 per cent in terms of employee satisfaction, as determined by attitude surveys, also performed better against a number of indicators, including absence. Table 3 shows the relative performances of the highest and lowest 20 per cent of units on the basis of employee satisfaction:

Table 3

EMPLOYEE SATISFACTION AND PERFORMANCE MEASURES*

Indicator	Top 20%	Bottom 20%
Quality of service	98.5%	94.8%
Mail Centre performance	74.3%	68.6%
Delivery performance	80.6%	78.9%
Sickness absence	*4.5%*	*5.2%*
Accidents/1,000 employees/ month	5.0%	5.8%

* All Royal Mail figures for 1995–96.

An analysis of sick absence levels and employee satisfaction scores indicated that the factors which matter most in encouraging employees to come to work rather than take sick leave are

□ their treatment by the line manager
□ recognition of their work
□ their importance as an employee
□ the pride they felt in working for the Royal Mail.

The organisation agreed with its unions and subsequently introduced a three-stage attendance procedure. For staff not 'on trial' the stages are based on minimum national attendance standards and call for varying degrees of disciplinary action, including dismissal:

□ Stage 1 is triggered after four absences or 14 days' sick leave in a 12-month period.
□ Stage 2 is based on two absences or 10 days lost in any six-month period in the following 12 months.
□ Stage 3 is based on two absences or 10 days lost in any six month period during the 12-month period following a Stage 2 warning.

At each stage managers are expected to explore with the employee the reason for absence, and to offer the assistance of medical and support services. In 1996 some 3,366 warnings/dismissals were given by line managers.The vast bulk of these (71 per cent) were Stage 1 warnings; only 158 (5 per cent) of the total resulted in dismissal. At all stages, and in taking the decision to proceed through the process, line managers are expected to take full account of individual circumstances and individual histories. The overall operation of the procedure is monitored by analysing whether line managers do take action at the various trigger points.

Setting attendance standards are only part of encouraging people back to work. The organisation has a raft of other policies including home visits, rehabilitating staff into work, and offering flexible working arrangements where appropriate.

There is also a great deal of professional support in the form of occupational health services, physiotherapy, case conferences, health promotions, stress management courses and trauma support. Ultimately, generous pension benefits are available for staff who have to retire early on ill-health grounds.

Royal Mail plans to develop its policy of focusing on improving attendance in future by means of a number of initiatives aimed at improving health and safety at work, reviewing medical retirement procedures, benchmarking performance, and providing continued support to employees.

BIBLIOGRAPHY

ADVISORY, CONCILIATION, AND ARBITRATION SERVICE (ACAS). (1977) *Code of Practice on Disciplinary Practice and Procedures in Employment*. London, HMSO.

ADVISORY, CONCILIATION, AND ARBITRATION SERVICE (ACAS). (1988) *Discipline at Work*. London, ACAS.

ADVISORY, CONCILIATION, AND ARBITRATION SERVICE (ACAS). (1994) *Absence and Labour Turnover*. London, ACAS.

AIKEN O. (1996a) 'Ill-health dismissals'. *People Management*. 7 November. p.47.

AIKEN O. (1996b) 'Who pays what when your employee falls ill?' *People Management*. 21 November. pp.46–47.

ARKIN A. (1992) 'Conspicuous by their absence'. *PM Plus*. 3, 7, July. pp.20–21.

ARKIN A. (1993) 'The workforce who got sick of absenteeism'. *PM Plus*. 4, 11, November. pp.18–19.

ARKIN A. (1997) 'Behind the screens'. *People Management*. 3 April. pp.39–40.

BECKARD R. (1992) 'A model for the executive management of transformational change', in G. Salaman (ed.), *Human Resource Strategies*, London, Sage.

BRAVERMAN H. (1974) *Labour and Monopoly Capital*. New York, Monthly Review Press.

BUCHANAN D. (1989) 'Job enrichment is dead: long live high performance work design'. *Personnel Management*. May. pp.40–43.

BUCHANAN D. (1992) 'High performance: new boundaries of acceptability in worker control', in G. Salaman (ed.),

Human Resource Strategies, London, Sage.

BUCHANAN D. (1994) 'Principles and practice in work design', in K. Sisson (ed.), *Personnel Management: A comprehensive guide to theory and practice in Britain*. Oxford, Blackwell's.

CONFEDERATION OF BRITISH INDUSTRY (CBI). (1989) *Managing Absence*. London, CBI.

CBI/PERCOM (1993) *Too Much Time Out? CBI/Percom Survey on Absence from Work*. London, CBI.

CBI/HAY (1994) *People, Paybill and the Public Sector*. London, CBI.

CBI/CENTREFILE (1995) *Managing Absence: 1995 CBI/Centrefile Survey Results*. London, CBI.

CBI/BUPA/MCG (1997) *Managing Absence – In sickness and in health*. London, CBI.

CCH (1997) 'Disability discrimination', in *British Personnel Management*, Bicester, CCH Editions Limited.

DALTON D. R. and MESCH D. J. (1990) 'The impact of flexible scheduling on employee attendance and turnover'. *Administrative Science Quarterly*. 35. pp.370–387.

DRAGO R. and WOODEN M. (1992) 'The determinants of labour absence: economic factors and workgroup norms across countries'. *Industrial and Labor Relations Review*. 45, 4, July. pp.764–778.

EDWARDS P. K. and WHISTON C. (1989) 'Industrial discipline, the control of attendance and the subordination of labour: towards an integrated analysis'. *Work, Employment and Society*. Vol.3, No.1, March. pp.1–28.

EVANS A. (1991) *Computers and Personnel Systems*. London, IPM.

EVANS A. and ATTEW T. (1986) 'Alternatives to full-time permanent staff', in C. Curson (ed.), *Flexible Patterns of Work*, London, IPM.

FAIR H. (1992) *Personnel and Profit*. London, IPM.

FOWLER A. (1993) *Discipline*. London, IPM.

FOWLER A. (1997) 'Benchmarking'. *People Management*. 12 June. pp.39–40.

HACKMAN J. R. and OLDHAM G. R. *et al* (1975) 'A new strategy for job enrichment'. *California Management Review*. 17, 4. pp.57–71.

HARVEY J. *and* NICHOLSON N. (1993) 'Incentives and penalties as a means of influencing attendance: a study in the UK public sector'. *International Journal of Human Resource Management*. 4, 4. December.

HERZBERG F. (1966) *Work and the Nature of Man*. London, Staples Press.

HILL J. M. M. *and* TRIST E. L. (1953) 'A consideration of industrial accidents as a means of withdrawal from the work situation'. *Human Relations*. 6. pp.357–380.

HILL J. M. M. *and* TRIST E. L. (1955) 'Changes in accidents and other absences with length of service'. *Human Relations*. 8. pp.121–152.

HMSO (1988) *Mental Health at Work*. London, HMSO.

HUCZYNSKI A. A. *and* FITZPATRICK M. J. (1989) *Managing Employee Absence for a Competitive Edge*. London, Pitman.

INCOMES DATA SERVICES (IDS). (1991) *Sick Pay Schemes*. Study 475, February.

INCOMES DATA SERVICES (IDS). (1992) *Controlling Absence*. Study 498, January.

INCOMES DATA SERVICES (IDS). (1994a) 'Persistent absenteeism'. *IDS Brief*. No.516, May. pp.7–10.

INCOMES DATA SERVICES (IDS). (1994b) *Absence and Sick Pay Policies*. Study No.556, June.

INCOMES DATA SERVICES (IDS). (1994c) *Sickness and Disability*. Employment Supplement No.71, August.

INDUSTRIAL RELATIONS SERVICES (1994) 'Sickness absence monitoring and control: a survey of practice'. *Industrial Relations Review and Report*. No.568, September. pp.4–16.

INDUSTRIAL RELATIONS SERVICES (1995a) 'Sickness absence'. *Industrial Relations Law Bulletin*. October. pp.2–9.

INDUSTRIAL RELATIONS SERVICES (1995b) 'Survey of employers' redundancy practices'. *Employment Trends*. No.580, March.

INDUSTRIAL RELATIONS SERVICES (1997) 'Survey of flexible patterns of work'. *Employment Trends*. June.

INDUSTRIAL SOCIETY (1994) *Managing Attendance*. London, Industrial Society.

INDUSTRIAL SOCIETY (1997) *Maximising Attendance*. London,

Industrial Society.

LABOUR FORCE SURVEY (1997) *Labour Market Trends*. January.

LEWIN K. (1951) *Field Theory in Social Science*. New York, Harper & Row.

LEWIS D. (1994) *Essentials of Employment Law*. London, IPM.

LONG P. *and* HILL M. (1988) *Special Leave*. London, IPM.

NICHOLSON N. (1977) 'Absence behaviour and attendance motivation: a conceptual synthesis'. *Journal of Management Studies*. 14. pp.231–252.

RHODES S. R. *and* STEERS R. M. (1990) *Managing Employee Absenteeism*, Reading, Mass., Addison Wesley.

ROBBINS S. P. (1993) *Organisational Behaviour*. Englewood Cliffs, New Jersey, Prentice Hall.

ROETHLISBERGER F. J. *and* DICKSON W. J. (1939) *Management and the Worker*. Cambridge, Mass., Harvard University Press.

SCOTT K. D. *and* MARKHAM S. (1982) 'Absenteeism control methods: a survey of practices and results'. *Personnel Administrator*. June. pp.73–84.

STEERS R. M. *and* RHODES S. R. (1978) 'Major influences on employee attendance: a process model'. *Journal of Applied Psychology*. 63, 4. pp.391–407.

STEERS R. M. *and* RHODES S. R. (1984) 'Knowledge and speculation about absenteeism', in P. S. Goodman and R. S. Atkin (eds), *Absenteeism: New Approaches to Understanding, Measuring and Managing Absence*. San Francisco, Jossey Bass.

SYRETT M. (1993) 'The best of everything'. *Human Resources*. Winter. pp.83–86.

TAYLOR F. W. (1911) *The Principles of Scientific Management*. New York, Harper.

TRIST E. L. *et al* (1963) *Organisational Choice*. London, Tavistock.

WARR P. *and* YEARTA S. (1995) 'Health and motivational factors in sickness absence'. *Human Resource Management Journal*. 5, 5. pp.33–48.

WICKENS P. (1987) *The Road to Nissan: Quality, Flexibility and Teamwork*. London, Macmillan.

INDEX

Other titles in this series

360-Degree Feedback

Peter Ward

Traditional performance appraisal involves bosses assessing their staff. Yet the people who actually work with us – peers, subordinates, suppliers and customers – can often provide far more accurate and useful insights into our strengths, weaknesses and scope for development ...

Organisations tap into these vital sources of information through 360-degree feedback, a process originally developed by NASA to evaluate their space programmes. In this pioneering book, consultant Peter Ward – who introduced the technique into Tesco – explains its advantages over other assessment methods and offers detailed practical guidance on implementation. He examines in turn:

- □ where, why and how to adopt 360-degree approaches
- □ designing, customising or buying in questionnaires
- □ planning, piloting and validating a new project
- □ transforming raw data into effective reports
- □ presenting the results and facilitating change
- □ issues of confidentiality and the link with reward
- □ lessons in best practice from leading organisations such as the AA, Arco, National Grid and Total.

Introducing 360-degree feedback can loosen up a rigid corporate culture and cast light on the vital process factors – teamwork, communications, decision-making and morale – that underlie long-term business success. The essential principles are set out in this book.

0 85292 705 3
1997
£18.99

I.T. Answers to H.R. Questions

Peter Kingsbury

Information technology can transform the quality of decision-making in HR departments. Yet far too many practitioners and students still lack the confidence and expertise to embrace its immense potential...

Data kept passively as hard copy is at best a necessary evil; but when the same information forms part of a flexible and dynamic datastore, it can streamline all the key personnel processes and feed in to powerful, action-oriented reports. In this concise, clearly argued and comprehensive text, Peter Kingsbury examines how to set up relational databases and computerised applications, and the best ways for IT to add value in:

- recruitment and selection
- the ongoing employment of staff
- performance management and appraisal
- identifying and assessing competencies
- business, career and succession planning
- training and development
- forecasting and controlling budgets.

Not even the best expert systems, admits Kingsbury, can yet take our HR decisions for us, but IT can reduce the routine for all personnel practitioners and enable them to make a far more strategic contribution to their businesses. His book sets out from first principles to demonstrate how this works.

0 85292 693 6
1997
£18.99

Appraisal:
Routes to improved performance

Clive Fletcher

Far from being just a meaningless form-filling exercise, appraisal can be one of the vital tools in harnessing employee commitment and managing performance.

In this acclaimed book, Professor Clive Fletcher examines aims and objectives; the uses of appraisal in motivation, assessment and development; and the best methods of designing, introducing, monitoring and maintaining systems. Now, taking full account of the latest trends and research findings, he has added a major new chapter on 360-degree techniques and extended his coverage of diversity, competence-based interviews and training, and feedback skills. Real-life examples from a wide variety of organisations enhance the argument throughout. Invaluable sample material – an external assessment report, a self-appraisal form, appraisers' and appraisees' notes, an interview feedback form and evaluation questionnaires – completes an ideal introductory text.

It succeeds admirably...well-written and very practical...I strongly recommend it as a guide through the minefield of appraisal – Paul Watkinson, Group Personnel Director, British Rail

A brief, readable book we should all read – Journal of Strategic Management

Second Edition
0 85292 690 1
1997
£18.99

New additions to the Developing Practice Series

Flexible Working Practices: Techniques and innovations
John Stredwick and Steve Ellis

Flexible working practices can make the difference between survival and success. Introducing flexible working practices can help organisations respond effectively to customer demand, cope with peaks and troughs in activity, recruit and retain the best people, and save significant sums of money. John Stedwick and Steve Ellis build on the experiences of leading-edge companies – from SmithKline Beecham to Simens GEC, Birds Eye to Xerox, Cable and Wireless to the Co-operative Bank – to help practitioners develop effective policies on:

- temporal flexibility: annual hours, job sharing, part-time and portfolio working
- predicting and unpredictable: complementary workers, interim managers and new forms of shiftworking
- functional flexibility: multiskilling, outsourcing, teleworking and call centres
- using individual and team reward – competence-based, performance-based and profit-related pay, and gainsharing and broadbanding – to support flexibility
- 'family-friendly' policies: flexitime, career breaks, childcare and elder-care
- clarifying the 'psychological contract' with empowered employees.

A closing chapter pulls together the different options and sets out the main techniques for 'selling' flexibility to a sceptical workforce.

0 85292 744 4
1998
£18.99

Performance Management: The new realities

Angela Baron and Michael Armstrong

All employers need to find ways to improve the performance of their people. Yet many of today's personnel departments are abolishing rigid systems of performance management in favour of strategic frameworks that empower individual managers to communicate with, motivate and develop their staff. Here, one of Britain's best-known business writers and the CIPD's policy adviser for employee resourcing draw on detailed data from over 550 organisations – including the latest innovations adopted by leading-edge companies, ranging from BP Exploration to the Corporation of London, and from AA Insurance to Zeneca – to illuminate how approaches to appraisal have evolved and to identity current best practice in performance management. They explore its history, philosophy and separate elements, the criticisms it has attracted and its impact (if any) on quantifiable business results. They also offer practitioners invaluable guidance on:

- the fundamental processes: from target-setting through measurement to performance and development reviews
- performance management skills: coaching, counselling and problem-solving
- meeting developmental needs and enhancing team performance
- paying for performance and compentences
- introducing performance management and evaluating its effectiveness.

Throughout, the authors have tailored their suggestions to the practical problems revealed by their research. There could be not better source of support for organisations facing this most crucial challenge.

0 85292 727 4
1998
£18.99